The

Southern

MOUNTAIN

Kitchen

BAKING

COOKBOOK

C.W.
Mullins

Light Of The Moon Publishing

ISBN: 978-1-958221-17-4

Printed in the United States of America

First Printing

Light Of The Moon has allowed this work to remain exactly as
the author intended, verbatim, without editorial input.

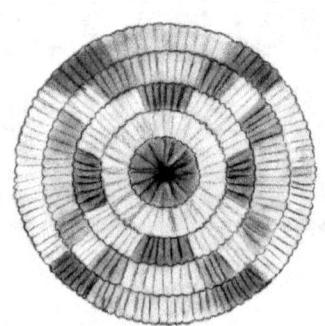

Visit G.W. Mullins for weekly cooking videos on The Southern Mountain Kitchen YouTube Channel:

https://www.youtube.com/@thesouthernmountainkitchen

And the Southern Mountain Kitchen Blog:

https://thesouthernmountainkitchen.blogspot.com/

Also Available from G.W. Mullins creator of
The Southern Mountain Kitchen

The Southern Mountain Kitchen Cookbook
Hardback ISBN: 978-1-958221-06-8 and Paperback ISBN:
978-1-958221-07-5. Available worldwide wherever great
books are sold.

This book is dedicated to the women who inspired it, my mother Marjorie and my great grandmother Myrtle. Without them, I would have never wanted to cook. When cooking many of these recipes, I am reminded how much I miss and love them both.

When you think about Southern food, it has a style and taste all its own. Then when you mix it with Mountain dishes, you have the most amazing result. The mix is like a party of flavor. In this book, I have tried to capture a collection of that amazing flavor, in a mix of baking recipes from my life on the mountain.

I was born Native American (Cherokee). Mix that with the variety of people who influenced the food on the mountain, from German, to French, to Italian and Polish. There were so many styles blended into our community, and that, I think made the foods we ate so amazing.

In this book, I have traveled back to a time when life was a little less complicated, when we all came together to enjoy a meal, as family and friends. I think that is why I choose to create food, to bring back a time when life was all about, family, friends and food.

In this baking collection, I include recipes for cakes, cookies, baked breads, cobblers and baked food dishes. Along the way, I even through in a few non baking dishes that I think you might enjoy. I hope you enjoy!

Table Of Contents

Breads, Rolls & Biscuits

G.W.'S FLAKEY SOUTHERN BISCUITS

2 ½ cups all-purpose flour
2 tsp. baking powder
½ tsp. baking soda
¾ tsp. salt
½ tsp sugar
1 stick butter
¼ cup shortening
1 cup buttermilk

Add to a large bowl flour, baking powder, baking soda, salt, sugar and mix together.

Add to bowl butter and shortening, then work the mix together with a fork. Break up butter and shortening until the bits resemble grains of rice in the flour.

Add buttermilk to bowl and mix into bowl.

Move mixed dough over to a cutting board coated with flour.

Roll out to thickness desired and use a biscuit cutter to cut biscuits.

Bake in oven at 425 degrees for around 20 to 25 minutes or until tops are browned.

SOURDOUGH STARTER

2 1/2 cups oil-purpose flour
1 pkg. active dry yeast
2 1/2 cups warm water
1 tbsp. honey

Mix all the ingredients, Let stand, uncovered, in a glass or crockery jar at room temperature for 24 hours. Cover; let stand about 3 days or until sour. Stir occasionally (time depends on room temperature). Dough will sour foster in a warm room.

To replenish starter, odd equal ports oil-purpose flour and water to equal total amount removed, Between use, keep covered in refrigerator. To keep several weeks or more, add 1 teaspoon sugar weekly.

When using sourdough for your bread recipes, for an average family, it is usually always a cup of sourdough starter.

GRANDMA'S DINNER ROLLS

1 ⅓ cups lukewarm water or milk
2 packets rapid rise yeast
1 tsp. sugar for yeast to feed off of
4 ½ cups of flour
1 large egg
5 tbsp. of melted butter
1 tsp. of salt
¼ cup of sugar

Add warm water to a bowl, pour in 1 tsp. of sugar, add two packet of Rapid Rise Yeast and mix with spatula. Allow to rise for about 5 minutes and yeast is frothy.

Add flour, salt, butter, sugar, and yeast mix to stand mixer with a dough hook. Mix until the ingredients combine together and form a ball around the hook.

Grease a large bowl with oil and transfer the dough to greased bowl. Cover with plastic, and place in a warm area to rise for at least an hour.

After an hour punch down the dough.

Prepare baking pans by lining with aluminum foil, with just a bit sticking off the edges, so the rolls can be removed with this later. Spray pans with cooking spray.

Pinch off bits if dough for your rolls and twist the sides down to the bottom and place in the pan.

When rolls are in pans, cover with plastic and allow to rise another 20 minutes.

Once rolls have risen again, brush with butter and place in over.

Bake at 400 degrees for 20 to 25 minutes or until browned.

Remove rolls from oven, and brush tops with butter again.

Allow rolls to sit for 5 minutes before removing from pan.

MILK AND HONEY WHOLE WHEAT BREAD

(makes 3 loaves)

3 cup warm water
½ cup oil or melted butter
2 cups instant dry milk
2 tbsp. baking yeast
½ cup honey
7 to 8 cups whole wheat flour
2 tsp. salt

Dissolve the yeast in the warm water. Add the oil and then the honey by measuring the oil first.

Stir the dry milk and 3 cups of the whole wheat flour together. Add this mixture to this liquid.

Beat the batter about 150 strokes (always beat in only one direction).

Cover the container and put in a warm place to rise for about an hour.

Beat in one direction again, then add the salt and gradually the rest of the flour until it is too stiff to beat.

Place the dough on a floured surface and knead. Add the rest of the flour as you knead. When the dough springs bock to the touch, it is ready to be formed into loaves; roll in vegetable oil for a good crust.

Let rise again to about double in size. Bake at 350 degrees F. for 30 minutes.

MAYONNAISE BISCUITS

2 cups self-rising flour
1 cup milk
4 tbsp. mayonnaise

Combine all ingredients. Mix well. Pour in a greased
muffin pan. Bake at 450 degrees F. For 15 to 20 minutes.

MAYONNAISE BISCUITS (2nd version)

1 cup self-rising flour
1 tbsp. mayonnaise
2 cups sweet milk

Mix together and spoon into muffin tins. Fill muffin tin 3/4
full. Bake at 425 degrees F. For 10 to 15 minutes. Makes 6
biscuits. Just increase quantities For more.

ANGEL BISCUITS

Sift together:

5 cups flour
3 tsp. baking powder
4 tsp. sugar
1 tsp. soda
2 tsp. salt

Add 1 cup cooking oil and cut into the dry mixture.
Dissolve 1 package dry yeast in 2 tablespoons warm water;
add 2 cups buttermilk and make into dough. Refrigerate
overnight or longer. Roll and cut as for biscuits. Dip into

melted butter and let stand I hour. Bake at 450 to 475 degrees F. until done.

CORN BREAD

Delicious right from oven.

1 cup sifted all-purpose flour
¼ cup sugar
4 tsp. baking powder
¾ tsp. salt
1 cup yellow cornmeal
2 eggs
1 cup milk
¼ cup cooking oil

Into mixer bowl, sift together flour, sugar, baking powder and salt; stir in cornmeal.

Add eggs, milk and oil.   Beat with mixer just until smooth, about 1 minute (do not over beat).

Pour into greased 9 x 9 x 2-inch baking pan. Bake in 425 degrees oven for 20 to 25 minutes.

Makes 8 to 9 servings.

CORN BREAD (version 2)

3 eggs
1 can cream style corn
½ cup corn oil
1 carton sour cream
2 pkg. Martha White corn meal mix

Stir all ingredients together and put in square cake pan.

Bake at 450 degrees for 30 minutes.

ICEBOX ROLLS

(This recipe is a started for when you need to prepare in advance.)

You need:

1 ¼ cup of boiling water

Add:

¼ cup sugar
2 tbsp. shortening
½ tsp. salt

Let cool.

Add to:

¼ cup tepid water
1 pack of yeast
¼ cup sugar

1 beaten egg
4 ½ to 5 cups flour

Add all ingredients to cool water and beat smooth. Pour in greased bowl and cover.

Place in icebox and use as needed. Will keep several days.

When ready to bake, preheat oven to 375 degrees. Brush rolls with melted butter; bake until golden brown, 15-20 minutes. Remove from oven; brush with more butter.

PUMPKIN BREAD

2 ¾ cups sugar
3 eggs
1 cup butter

Beat together above ingredients and add:

2 cups pumpkin
½ tsp. baking powder
1 tsp. nutmeg
1 tsp. baking soda
3 ½ cups flour
1 tsp. cloves
1 tsp. allspice

Combine all ingredients, mixing well and place into 2 well-greased and floured loaf pans.

Bake at 325 degrees for 1 hour and 15 minutes, or until toothpick inserted in center comes out clean.

JIFFY HOT ROLLS

2 cups self-rising flour
1 cup milk
4 tbsp. mayonnaise
2 tbsp. sugar

Stir and spoon in muffin pan. Bake at 350 for about 20 minutes.

This makes about 12 rolls.

HERBED BISCUIT RING

3 tbsp. margarine
1 tsp. lemon juice
dash paprika
1 tsp. sesame seed
¼ tsp. dried thyme, crushed
⅛ tsp. rubbed sage
1 pkg. (10) refrigerated biscuits

Blend together margarine, lemon juice, paprika, sesame seed, thyme and sage. Separate biscuits; spread tops with herb margarine.

In 8 x 11/2-inch round layer pan, arrange biscuits, margarine side up, to form ring, overlapping slightly.

Bake in 400-degree oven for 15 to 18 minutes or until golden.

Makes 10 servings.

BANANA BREAD

1 cup. sugar
½ cup shortening
2 eggs
1 ⅓ cups mashed bananas
2 ½ cups sifted flour
1 tsp. baking soda
½ tsp. salt
¾ cup nuts

Cream sugar and shortening; add beaten eggs, then bananas.

Sift flour, salt and baking soda together; add to first mixture. Add nuts.

Bake in 350-degree oven about 45 minutes.

GINGER BREAD

1 cup brown sugar
½ cup butter
1 cup molasses
2 tsp. baking soda
1 cup boiling water

Mix well.

3 cups flour
½ tsp. salt
1 tsp. each: ginger, cinnamon, cloves, allspice, nutmeg

Add last - 2 well beaten eggs.

Bake 30 minutes at 350 F. degrees.

Top with raisins, candy, fruit or chocolate icing.

BROWN BREAD

2 cups buttermilk
¼ cup dark molasses
1 cup raisins
1 cup whole wheat flour
l cup rye flour
1 cup yellow cornmeal
¾ tsp. baking soda
½ tsp. salt
boiling water

In a large mixing bowl, blend together buttermilk and molasses. Stir in raisins.

Thoroughly stir together whole wheat flour, rye flour, cornmeal, baking soda and salt. Stir into buttermilk mixture until blended.

Divide batter among 3 greased 20-ounce clean cans. (Or 4 (16 ounce) cans.) Cover cans tightly with foil; place on rack set in large Dutch oven.

Pour boiling water into Dutch oven to a depth of l inch. Cover and simmer over low heat, steaming bread until done, 2 ½ - 3 hours.

Add more boiling water as needed.

Remove bread from cans and cool on a rack.

Makes 3 - 4 loaves.

SPIDER CORN BREAD

1 ⅓ cup white cornmeal
⅓ cup sifted flour
1 tsp. baking soda
½ tsp. salt
¼ cup sugar
1 cup buttermilk
2 eggs, well beaten
2 cups milk
2 tbsp. butter

Place cornmeal, flour, baking soda, salt and sugar in mixing bowl and mix.

Add buttermilk, eggs and 1 cup milk. Beat until smooth.

Melt butter in skillet and when hot, pour in batter.

Slowly and carefully pour last cup of milk over top of batter,

Bake at 350 degrees for about 50 minutes or until corn bread is lightly browned on top.

DUTCH OVEN CORN BREAD

¼ cup melted butter
2 eggs
1 tbsp. sugar
1 tsp. salt
3 tsp. baking powder
1 ½ cups milk
2 cups flour
1 cup cornmeal

Melt butter, Combine dry ingredients in large bowl. Beat eggs and milk together and pour over dry ingredients. Stir until smooth, then add melted butter and stir until well mixed.

Pour into a buttered Dutch oven - the batter should not be more than 1 1/2 inches deep - and cover.

Place the Dutch oven into heated stove oven at 350 degrees.

It should bake in about 25 - 30 minutes. Check it after about 20 minutes. It is done when a sharp knife placed into the center comes out clean.

PEPPERONI BREAD

1 pkg. frozen bread dough (2 loaves)
1 pkg. pepperoni slices
2 bell peppers
½ lb. provolone cheese
grated Parmesan cheese

Grate cheese and thaw bread dough.

Fry peppers in 2 tablespoons oil. Cool.

Roll dough to measure 12 x 2.4 inches.

Arrange down the center of dough lengthwise, a layer of cheese, pepperoni, peppers, and sprinkle with Parmesan cheese.

Add a sprinkle of garlic salt to taste.

Fold the sides of the dough over the filling and seal well.

Brush top with oil from the peppers.

Bake at 350 degrees F. until golden brown, about 25 minutes.

CORNBREAD 3

Sift together:

1 cup flour
¾ tsp. baking soda
1 tsp. salt
1 tsp. baking powder

Add 1 ½ cups cornmeal.

Combine:

2 eggs, well beaten
2 tbsp. brown sugar
½ cup melted shortening (bacon drippings are best)

Add eggs, sugar, and shortening to 1 ½ cups buttermilk, then add to dry ingredients. Beat only until moist.

Bake in well-oiled pan or iron skillet at 450 degrees F, until golden brown.

QUICK BUTTERMILK ROLLS

1 cup warm buttermilk
3 tbsp. sugar
2 ½ cups self-rising flour
1 pkg. dry yeast (put in buttermilk)
3 tbsp. melted shortening

Roll out like biscuits, cut out, and dip in butter.

Let rise 15 to 20 minutes and bake at 450 degrees F.

BUTTERMILK CRESCENTS

3 ¼ cups un-sifted flour
½ cup buttermilk
2 tbsp. sugar
½ cup water
1 tsp. salt
¼ cup margarine
⅛ tsp. baking soda
melted margarine
1 pkg. active dry yeast

Combine 1 cup flour, sugar, salt, baking soda, and yeast.

Heat buttermilk, water, and margarine to 120 to 130 degrees F.

Add to dry ingredients; beat 2 minutes at medium speed.

Add ½ cup flour.

Beat at high speed 2 minutes. Stir in more flour to make a soft dough.

On floured board, knead 8 to 10 minutes.

Place in greased bowl; grease top. Cover; let rise until doubled, about 1 hour. Punch down.

On floured board, roll into 2 circles 12 inches in diameter. Brush with margarine. Cut each into 12 pre-shaped pieces.

Roll up each piece. Seal points firmly. Place on greased baking sheets, points underneath, 2 inches apart. Curve to form crescents. Cover; let rise until doubled, about 1 hour,

Bake at 375° F. for 10 to 15 minutes. While hot, brush with margarine.

Makes two dozen rolls.

POTATO ROLLS

1 cup milk
2 tbsp. sugar
2 tsp. salt
¼ cup (½ stick) margarine
1 cup warm water (105 to 115 degrees F.)
1 pkg. active dry yeast
2 eggs, beaten
1 cup instant potato flakes
4 ½ - 5 ½ cups un-sifted flour

Scald milk; stir in sugar, salt, and margarine. Cool to lukewarm.

Measure warm water into large warm bowl. Sprinkle in yeast; stir until dissolved.

Stir in lukewarm milk mixture, eggs, instant potatoes, and 3 cups flour. Beat until smooth.

Stir in enough additional flour to make a slightly stiff dough. Turn dough out onto lightly floured board; knead until smooth and elastic, about 8 minutes.

Place in greased bowl, turning to grease top, Cover; let rise in warm place, free from draft, until doubled in size, about 1 hour.

Punch dough down; turn out onto lightly floured board. Divide dough in half and divide each half into 12 equal pieces, form into smooth balls.

Place in 2 greased 9-inch round cake pans. Cover and let rise in warm place, free from draft, until doubled in size, about 30 minutes.

Bake at 400 degrees F. for about 20 minutes, or until done.

Remove from pans and cool on wire racks.

Makes two dozen rolls.

COTTAGE CHEESE ROLLS

Combine the following:

1 pkg. dry yeast
¼ tsp. baking powder
1 ⅓ cups all-purpose flour, sifted

Heat the next ingredients together until butter melts:

1 cup creamed cottage cheese
¼ cup water
2 tbsp. sugar
1 tbsp. butter
1 tsp. salt

Add above to dry ingredients.

Add 1 egg. Beat at low speed for ½ minute. Beat 3 minutes at high speed.

Stir in 1 cup more of flour.

Pour in greased bowl, turning once. Let rise till doubled, 1 1/2 hours.

Divide into 12 rolls in well-greased muffin tins. Let rise 40 minutes.

Bake in 400 degrees F. oven for 12 to 15 minutes.

You can add 2 teaspoons caraway seed and two teaspoons grated onion and have caraway puffs.

Make sure dough does not over rise or under rise.

HOMEMADE BREAD

1 pkg, yeast
¼ cup lukewarm water
2 cups milk, scalded
3 tbsp. sugar
1 tbsp. salt
3 tbsp. shortening
about 5 cups sifted, all-purpose flour

Dissolve yeast in water. Add sugar, salt, and shortening to hot milk. Cool until lukewarm.

Then stir in two cups of flour. Add softened yeast. Add just enough more flour to make a moderately stiff dough.

Turn out on a lightly floured board or cloth. Cover dough with a bowl and let rise 10 minutes. Knead dough until smooth, 5 to 10 minutes.

Shape dough into a ball and place in a lightly greased bowl, turning greased side up. Cover and let rise in a warm place until doubled, about 1 ½ hours.

Punch dough down and let rest 10 minutes. Divide dough in half and shape into two loaves. Place shaped loaves in greased bread pans.

Brush tops with melted shortening. Let rise in warm place until about 2 inches over top of pan (about 1 hour).

Place on low rack in a 425 degree F. oven and bake 35 minutes; if using a glass pan, bake at 400 degrees F.

Turn bread out on racks to cool.

Makes 2 loaves of bread.

BEER BREAD

3 cups all-purpose flour
½ tsp. baking soda
3 tbsp. sugar
1 tsp. baking powder
1 can of beer
2 tbsp. butter, melted

Mix all ingredients and pour into greased 9 x 5 x 3 loaf pan.

Bake at 325 degrees for 50 minutes.
Remove from oven. slit top and pour in some melted butter.

Return to oven for 10 more minutes.

Yield: 1 loaf.

CRANBERRY NUT BREAD

2 cups whole wheat flour
2 cups all-purpose flour
1 tbsp. baking powder
1 tbsp. baking soda
1 tsp. salt
½ tsp. cinnamon
¼ tsp. nutmeg
1 cup brown sugar
1 cup sugar
½ cup margarine
1 tbsp. grated orange rind
1½ cups orange juice
2 eggs
2 cups fresh cranberries, cut in half
1 cup chopped nuts
⅔ cup raisins

Sift dry ingredients into mixing bowl. Cut in margarine until mixture resembles coarse cornmeal; set aside.

Combine orange rind, juice and eggs. Add all at once, to dry ingredients.

Mix just until dry ingredients are moistened. Fold in nuts and raisins. Pour into 2 oiled and floured, 8 x 4 x 3-inch loaf pans.
Bake at 350 degrees for 1 hour.

Cool in pans for 10 minutes, then remove from pans and cool completely on wire racks.

Yield: 2 loaves.

Note: Nice bread for the holiday season. Keeps well.

SPOON BREAD

1½ cups boiling water
1 tbsp. margarine
1 cup white or yellow cornmeal
1 egg, beaten
¾ tsp. salt
1 cup buttermilk
1 tsp. baking soda

Combine water and cornmeal and beat until well blended.

Add remaining ingredients; mix.

Pour into a hot greased, 7-inch baking dish.

Bake at 350 degrees for 30 minutes or until toothpick inserted in center of pan comes out clean.

Serve hot with butter and honey.

Yield: 4 to 6 servings.

Note: if you wish to keep the top soft, add a few tablespoons milk while the bread is baking.

STRAWBERRY BREAD

2 cups sugar
4 eggs
1 tsp. baking soda
1 tsp. salt
2 (10-ounce) packages of fresh or frozen strawberries
3 tsp. cinnamon
3 cups all-purpose flour
1¼ cups oil
1½ cups chopped pecans

Using electric mixer, in a large bowl, combine sugar, eggs, strawberries, cinnamon, baking soda, salt, flour, oil and mix well.

Then, add pecans.

Put into two well buttered 8 x 4 x 3 loaf pans and bake at 350 degrees for 1 hour.

Yield: 2 loaves.

OLD FASHIONED PAN BREAD

2 cups self-rising flour
1 pinch baking soda
⅛ cup shortening
4 tbsp. grated cold butter
1 - 1 ½ cups whole buttermilk

Add flour and baking soda to bowl.

Blend in shortening with fork until shortening is about pea size.

Grate butter into bowl. Use the fork to toss together well.

Add buttermilk. Mixture should be wet.

Pour into a VERY well-greased 10" iron skillet.

Grease skillet with shortening.

Bake at 450 degrees until good and brown. About 30 minutes.

Flip upside down and cut in triangles like you would cornbread.

Cakes

BANANA PUDDING CAKE

1 or 2 small bananas
1 pkg. yellow cake mix
1 pkg. Jell-o brand instant Banana Cream Pudding
4 eggs
1 cup water
¼ cup oil
½ cup nuts (optional), chopped

Slice bananas and beat well; add remaining ingredients and beat 2 minutes or until smooth.

Bake 60 to 70 minutes in a greased and floured tube pan at 350 degrees.

Sprinkle with confectioners' sugar, if desired.

VANILLA WAFER CAKE

1 cup butter
2 cups sugar
½ cup milk
6 eggs
7 oz. box angel flake coconut
1 box (12 oz.) vanilla wafers
dash of salt
1 cup nuts (1/2 cup pecans, 1/2 cup black walnuts)
1 tsp. vanilla
1 tsp. baking powder

Add butter, sugar, milk, baking powder, salt and vanilla. Mix together then add I egg at a time; add vanilla wafers, nuts and coconut.

Grease cake pan. Line with wax paper.

Bake 2 hours at 275 degrees.

CARROT CAKE

4 eggs
2 cups sugar
1 ¼ cups oil
1 tsp. baking soda
1 tsp. baking powder
½ tsp. salt
2 tsp. cinnamon
2 cups flour
3 cups grated carrots

Beat eggs and sugar together; then add oil.

Sift the dry ingredients, and then add.

Grate and add carrots last.

Bake at 300 degrees for about 40 minutes in layer cake pans or 1 1/2 hours if baked in oblong pan.

Icing:

Cream together:

8 oz. pkg. cream cheese
1 stick butter

Add 1 box powdered sugar, gradually beating with mixer to a creamy consistency.

Add:

1 cup chopped pecans
2 tsp. lemon juice

SOUR CREAM COFFEE CAKE

1 stick butter or margarine
1 cup sugar
2 eggs, beaten
1 cup sour cream
2 cups sifted flour
2 tsp. baking powder
1 tsp. soda
⅛ tsp salt
1 tsp. vanilla

Cream butter and sugar. Add eggs and vanilla. Mix well. Alternately add sour cream and dry ingredients.

Mix together:

¾ cup brown sugar
½ cup chopped nuts
½ tsp. cinnamon

Pour ½ batter in greased pan, then half of topping and repeat layers.

Bake at 350 degrees for 40 - 50 minutes.

Drizzle with vanilla icing, if desired.

BLUE RIBBON CARROT CAKE

2 cups all-purpose flour
2 tsp. baking soda
½ tsp. salt
2 tsp. cinnamon
3 eggs, well beaten
¾ cup vegetable oil
¾ cup buttermilk
2 cups sugar
2 tsp. vanilla
1 (8-ounce) can crushed pineapple, drained
2 cups carrots, grated
1 (3½-ounce) can flaked coconut
1 cup walnuts, chopped
Buttermilk Glaze (recipe included at end)
Orange & Cream Cheese Frosting (recipe included at end)

Combine flour, baking soda, salt, and cinnamon; set aside.

Combine eggs, oil, buttermilk. sugar and vanilla; beat until smooth.

Stir in flour mixture, pineapple, carrots, coconut and chopped walnuts.

Pour batter into 2 greased and floured 9-inch round cakepans.

Bake at 350 degrees for 35 to 40 minutes or until a butterknife inserted in center comes out clean.

Immediately spread Buttermilk Glaze evenly over layers. Cool in pans 15 minutes, then remove from pans, and let cool completely.

Spread Orange-Cream Cheese Frosting between layers and on top and sides of cake. Store cake in refrigerator.

Yield: one 2-layer cake.

Buttermilk Glaze:

1 cup sugar
½ tsp. baking soda
½ cup buttermilk
½ cup butter
1 tbsp. light corn syrup
1 tbsp. vanilla

Combine sugar, baking soda, buttermilk. butter, and corn syrup in a Dutch oven. Bring to a boil: cook 4 minutes, stirring often. Remove from heat and stir In vanilla. Yield: about 1½ cups.

Orange & Cream Cheese Frosting:

½ cup butter, softened
2 cups powdered sugar, sifted
1 (8 ounce) package cream cheese, softened
1 tsp. orange juice
1 tsp. grated orange rind
1 tsp. vanilla extract

Combine butter and cream cheese, beating until light and fluffy. Add vanilla, powdered sugar, juice and rind: beat until smooth.

Yield: frosting for one 2-layer cake.

COCONUT CAKE

1 (18½-ounce) box white cake mix
1 (7-ounce) can coconut
1 (15-ounce) can coconut cream
1 (9-ounce) carton frozen, non-dairy whipped topping

Add 1/2 can coconut to cake mix: prepare according to directions on box and bake in a 13 x9 x 2-inch pan.

While cake is still warm. punch holes in with a toothpick and pour the coconut cream over it.

Cool completely and ice with whipped topping. Sprinkle remaining coconut over cake and refrigerate.

Yield: 12 to 16 servings.

SWEETENED CONDENSED MILK POUND CAKE

1 lb. butter
2 cups sugar
8 egg yolks
3 ½ cups of flour
14 oz. sweetened condensed milk
8 egg whites

Preheat oven to 325F. Grease pan.

Cream together butter and sugar until fluffy.

Add in egg yolks one at a time. Alternate adding flour and condensed milk, scraping down sides occasionally.

In a separate bowl, whip egg whites until fluffy. Fold into mixture.

Put mix in greased pan and bake at 325 degrees F for 90 minutes.

BROWN SUGAR POUND CAKE

1 (16-ounce) box light brown sugar (2 ½ cups, packed)
1 cup sugar
1 ½ cups margarine
5 eggs
1 cup milk
1 tsp. vanilla
3 cups sifted all-purpose flour
½ tsp. baking powder
½ tsp. salt
1 cup chopped nuts

Combine sugars and margarine; beat until creamy.

Add eggs one at a time, beating well after each addition.

Combine milk and vanilla; set aside.

Mix dry ingredients by sifting. Add alternately with milk to creamed mixture.

Pour into a greased and floured tube pan.

Bake at 350 degrees for 1 hour 20 minutes or until a cake tester inserted in the middle of the cake comes out clean.

Yield: 10 to 12 servings.

CREAM CHEESE POUND CAKE

1½ cups margarine, softened
1 (8-ounce) package cream cheese, softened
6 eggs
3 cups sugar
3 cups all-purpose flour
1 tsp. baking powder
2 tsp. vanilla
2 tsp. lemon extract

Cream margarine and cream cheese in mixing bowl until smooth and fluffy.

Add eggs 1 at a time, beating well after each additional.

Mix in remaining ingredients.

Pour into a well-oiled and floured, 10-inch, tube pan

Bake at 350 degrees for 1 ½ hours. Cool on a wire rack.

Yield: 10 to 12 servings.

POUND CAKE

1 lb. butter, creamed
1 lb. sugar
10 eggs
1 tbsp. vanilla extract
1 tbsp. lemon extract
1 lb. flour

Cream butter and sugar; add eggs, one at a time, and beat, Add vanilla or lemon flavorings to flavor.

Pour into tube pan. Bake 2 hours at 250 degrees F.

POUND CAKE 2

Cream together:

3 cups sugar
3 sticks butter

Add:

5 eggs (one at a time)
1 cup canned milk
1/2 tsp. salt
3 cups all-purpose flour
1 tsp. vanilla
½ tsp. almond

Grease and flour tube pan.

Bake at 350 degrees F. for 1 ½ hours in preheated oven. Do not open oven door while baking,

WHITE POUND CAKE

Cream together:

1 cup shortening or butter
2 ½ cups sugar
2 cups sweet milk
2 tsp. baking powder
4 cups flour

Fold in:
6 egg whites
1 ½ tsp. vanilla

Bake in tube pan at 350 degrees F, for about 1 hour or until golden.

CHOCOLATE MOUND CAKE

1 box devil's food cake mix

Bake cake as directed on box, using 8- or 9-inch pans.
Let cake cool well.

Split each cake in half to make 4 layers.

Filling:

1 cup sweet milk
1 stick margarine or butter
20 large marshmallows
1 cup sugar
1 cup chopped nuts
1 (12 oz.) can coconut

Mix in saucepan, milk, sugar, margarine and nuts. Let mixture come to a boil,

Tum heat to low and add the marshmallows and coconut. Stir until marshmallows are melted. Cool for 8 minutes.

Spread between the split layers.

Icing:

1 box confectioners' sugar
1 stick margarine or butter
2 chocolate squares
¼ cup milk

Melt chocolate and margarine or butter. Remove from heat, add sugar and milk. Beat until smooth. Then ice as any other cake.

OLD FASHIONED STACK CAKE

1 cup shortening
1 cup sugar
1 egg
1 cup molasses
¼ cup buttermilk
4 cups flour
1 tsp. salt
1 tsp. baking soda
1 tsp. cinnamon
1 tsp. ginger

Beat shortening, sugar, molasses and egg together; add buttermilk and dry ingredients to make a stiff dough.

Press into cake pans to make 4 or 5 thin layers. Bake in 350 degrees F, oven until lightly brown.

When cool, put together with a thin layer of applesauce. It is better to set overnight to soften.

CHOCOLATE CAKE

1 cup sourdough starter
1 cup sugar
½ cup shortening
½ tsp. salt
1 cup evaporated milk
1 tsp. vanilla
1 tsp. cinnamon
3 (1 oz.) squares semi-sweet chocolate
1 ½ tsp. baking soda
2 cups flour
2 eggs

Cream sugar and shortening until light and fluffy.

Beat in eggs, one at a time.

Stir in sourdough starter, milk, vanilla, cinnamon and melted chocolate. Beat with a mixer for 2 minutes.

Blend salt and baking soda together until smooth. Sprinkle over batter and fold in gently. Fold in flour until batter is smooth.

Pour into greased and floured cake pans. Bake at 350 degrees F. for 35 to 40 minutes. Cool and frost.

WHOOPEE PIES

1 cup shortening
2 cups sugar
2 eggs
1 cup sour milk
2 tsp. vanilla
2 cups whole wheat flour
2 tsp. salt
2 tsp. soda
½ to ¾ cup water

Cream shortening and sugar. Add eggs and beat. Add dry ingredients and liquid alternately and enough water to make dough.

Drop by teaspoon onto cookie sheet.

Bake 10 minutes at 350 degrees.

Cool and fill with:

1 tbsp. vanilla
4 cups confectioners' sugar
2 tbsp. milk
1 cup shortening
¼ cup wheat germ

Place filling between 2 cookies, making a sandwich.

Variations:
Add raisins and/or nuts to cookie batter.
Add wheat germ to batter.
Add chocolate to batter.

APPLE BUTTER CAKE

½ cup butter
1 cup sugar
4 eggs, beaten
2 ½ cups flour
1 ½ tsp. baking soda
1 tsp. cinnamon
¼ tsp. cloves
¼ tsp. nutmeg
1 cup buttermilk
1 cup apple butter

Cream shortening and sugar, add eggs.

Add dry ingredients alternately with buttermilk. Mix well.

Blend in apple butter.

Bake in square or loaf pan at 350° for 45 - 50 minutes.

APPLE BUTTER BUNDT CAKE

2 cups flour
1 cup sugar
1 tsp. baking soda
½ tsp. salt
1 tsp. cinnamon
½ tsp. nutmeg

Sift dry ingredients.

Add:

1 egg
3 oz. yogurt (plain)
1 cup apple butter
¼ cup oil
nuts and raisins

Bake at 350° for 1hour.

Sprinkle with confectioners' sugar

RHUBARB CAKE

Wash, drain and dice 2 cups rhubarb. Mix with 1/2 cup sugar and let stand.

½ cup shortening
1 ½ cups sugar
1 egg
1 cup buttermilk
1 tsp. vanilla
2 cups flour

1 tsp. baking soda
¼ tsp. salt
1 tsp. cinnamon

Cream shortening and sugar. Add egg, then sifted dry ingredients alternately with milk, Add vanilla and mix well.

Fold in rhubarb and stir well.

Bake 1 hour at 350° in greased pan.

Serve with whipped cream or ice cream.

ANGEL FOOD CAKE

1 cup cake flour
1 ½ cups sugar
1 ½ cups egg whites (approximately 10 to 12 eggs)
¾ tsp. salt
1 ½ tsp. cream of tartar
1 tsp. vanilla
¼ tsp. almond extract

Sift flour, measure. Add ¼ cup of the sugar to the flour and sift together three times.

Beat egg whites to a coarse foam at high speed; sprinkle salt and cream of tartar over the surface and continue beating until stiff but glossy.

Continue beating at low speed, adding remaining 1 ¼ cups sugar over surface, about 2 tablespoons at a time.

Add flavorings and finish beating by hand.

Gradually sift the flour and sugar mixture over egg whites, folding in only enough to blend.

Pour into ungreased 10-inch tube pan.

Bake at 275 degrees for 30 minutes, then at 325 degrees for 30 minutes more.

Invert on cake rack for about an hour before removing cake from pan.

Yield: 8 to 12 servings.

COCONUT LAYER CAKE

3 cups cake flour
2 tsp. baking powder
¼ tsp. salt
1 cup shortening
2 cups sugar
4 eggs, separated
2 tsp. vanilla
1 cup milk
1 cup heavy cream
1 cup shredded coconut

Sift flour once, measure; add baking powder and salt; sift together twice.

Cream shortening thoroughly; add sugar gradually; cream until light and fluffy.

Beat egg yolks until light and add to creamed mixture; blend well. Add vanilla.

Add dry ingredients alternately with milk, beating after each addition.

Beat egg whites until stiff but not dry, and fold into mixture.

Pour into 3 greased 9-inch layer cake pans and bake at 350 degrees for 25 minutes.

Remove cakes to racks and when thoroughly cool. Spread each layer with whipped cream, sweetened if desired, and sprinkle with shredded coconut.

Yield: 8 to 10 servings.

DUMP CAKE

1 lg. can crushed pineapple.
1 box white cake mix undrained
1 ½ sticks margarine
1 can cherry pie filling
Chopped nuts (opt.)

Mix pineapple and pie filling in bottom of 9 x 13-inch pan.

Sprinkle dry cake mix over fruit mixture.

Cut margarine into little pats and dot over dry cake mix.

Sprinkle nuts over top (if desired).

Bake at 350' for 30 minutes.

BANANA SPLIT CAKE

1 slick margarine, melted
2 cups graham cracker crumbs
1 (20-oz.) can crushed pineapple, drained
2 eggs
2 sticks margarine
2 cups powdered sugar
4 sliced bananas
1 (9-oz.) container nondairy topping
¾ cup chopped pecans
½ cup chopped maraschino cherries

Pour melted margarine over graham cracker crumbs; mix well.

Press into 9 x 13 x 2-inch pan.

Beat eggs, 2 sticks margarine and powdered sugar with electric mixer, no less than 15 minutes. Spread this mixture over crumbs in pan.

Next, layer sliced bananas, then drained pineapple and again bananas.

Cover all with nondairy topping. Sprinkle over nuts and maraschino cherries.

Refrigerate overnight.

ROOT BEER FLOAT CAKE

1 pkg. white cake mix
1¼ cup root beer
¼ cup vegetable oil
2 eggs

Heat oven to 350 degrees.

Generously grease and flour 13 x 9-inch pan.

Beat dry cake mix, root beef. oil and eggs on low speed 30
seconds. Beat on high speed 2 minutes.

Bake 30-40 minutes, until done.

Cool and serve with Root Beer Cream topping below.

Sprinkle with crushed root beer flavored hard candies, if
desired.

Root Beer Cream:

1 pkg. Dream Whip
½ cup chilled root beer

Beat all together on high 4 minutes or until thickened.

RAW APPLE CAKE

¼ cup cooking oil
2 cups sugar
3 eggs
3 cups flour
1 tsp. salt
1 tsp. baking soda
1 tsp. cinnamon
1 tsp. vanilla
3 cups raw apples, chopped
1 cup pecans or walnuts

Combine all ingredients and mix well. Bake at 350 degrees F. for 1 hour and 20 minutes.

Sauce:

½ cup buttermilk
1 stick margarine
1 cup sugar
1 tsp. vanilla
½ tsp. baking soda

Combine buttermilk, margarine, sugar, vanilla, and baking soda. Boil rapidly for 2 minutes, stirring constantly.

Pour over cake in pan while the cake is still hot.

Leave in pan for several hours before removing.

WEDDING CARROT CAKE

(Make this recipe double and bake in pans 13x9x2 inches.)

2 ½ cups flour
½ tsp. baking powder
2 tsp. baking soda
1 ½ tsp. cinnamon
½ tsp. salt
3 large eggs
1 cup sugar
½ cup vegetable oil
1 cup drained, crushed pineapple
2 tsp. vanilla
2 ½ cups coarsely grated carrots
½ cup shredded or flaked coconut
½ cup chopped pecans

Grease pans. Line bottom with waxed paper and flour them also. Remove excess flour.

Sift flour with soda, cinnamon, baking powder, and salt.

In large bowl, beat eggs with electric mixer at medium speed, until light and fluffy. Add sugar, oil, pineapple, and vanilla. Beat until blended. Reduce speed and add flour mixture, a third at a time, beating well after each addition. Fold in the carrots, coconut, and nuts.

Bake in center of oven at 350 degrees F. for 40 to 45 minutes. Cool for 5 minutes and ice. (continued next page)

WEDDING CAKE FROSTING
(for Wedding Carrot Cake)

Step 1:

3 tbsp, flour
1 cup water
⅛ tsp. salt

Cook these ingredients in saucepan on low heat until thick.

Step 2:

Cream together:

½ cup butter
½ cup shortening
1 cup sugar

Add mixture number 1 to mixture number 2 and beat rapidly until it looks like whipping cream.

Double if large cake is made.

MISSISSIPPI MUD CAKE AND FROSTING

2 sticks butter or margarine
½ cup cocoa
2 cups sugar
4 eggs, slightly beaten
1 ½ cups all-purpose flour
pinch of salt
1 ½ cups chopped nuts
1 tsp. vanilla
miniature marshmallows

Melt butter/margarine and cocoa together. Remove from heat and stir in sugar and beaten eggs. Mix well.

Add flour, salt, nuts, and vanilla. Mix well.

Spoon batter into a greased 13 x 9-inch pan.

Bake at 350 degrees F. for 35 to 45 minutes, until done.

Sprinkle on marshmallows (or marshmallow cream may be used) on top of warm cake. Frost.

Frosting:

1 box confectioners' sugar
½ cup milk
⅓ cup cocoa
½ stick butter or margarine softened

Combine sugar, cocoa, milk, and butter/margarine. Mix until smooth and spread on warm cake.

TUNNEL OF FUDGE CAKE

1 ½ cup butter
6 eggs
1 ½ cup sugar
2 cups flour
1 pkg. Fudge Buttercream frosting mix
2 cups chopped walnuts

Cream butter in large mixer bowl at high speed of mixer.
Add eggs one at a time, beating well after each.

Gradually add sugar and continue creaming at high speed
until light and fluffy.

By hand, stir in flour, frosting mix, and walnuts until
blended.

Pour batter into greased Bundt pan or 10-inch tube pan.
Bake at 350 degrees F. for 60 to 65 minutes.

Cool 2 hours; remove from pan, Cool completely before
serving.

Note: Nuts and frosting mix are essential to success of this
unusual recipe. Since cake has a soft fudgy interior, test for
doneness after 60 minutes by observing dry, shiny brownie
type crust.

HERSHEY BAR CAKE

½ lb. butter or margarine
1 cup sugar
4 eggs
2 tsp. vanilla
½ tsp. salt
1 tsp. vanilla
1-3 tbsp. hot water
8 plain Hershey bars, melted in double boiler, with 2 tbsp. water
1 ½ cups all-purpose flour
1 cup buttermilk
¼ tsp. baking soda
½ cup chopped nuts

Cream butter, sugar, add and beat eggs, one at a time into mixture.

Add vanilla, salt, and melted Hershey bars.

Add flour and buttermilk, with soda, alternately. Fold in nuts.

Bake in greased tube pan for 1 ¾ hours in 325-degree F. oven.

Sprinkle with powdered sugar when done.

CHERRY PINEAPPLE DUMP CAKE

1 can red cherry pie filling
1 can crushed pineapple with juice
1 box yellow cake mix
2 sticks butter, melted
1 can coconut
1 pkg. walnuts

Dump all ingredients in order as listed above, into pan or dish (ungreased). Do not stir. Bake at 350° F. for 1 hour.

Frosting:

Use 7 Minute Frosting. Cover icing with coconut.

7 Minute Frosting Recipe:

1 cup sugar
1/4 teaspoon salt
1/2 teaspoon cream of tartar
2 egg whites
3 tablespoons water
1 teaspoon vanilla extract

Combine all of the ingredients except the vanilla in a stainless steel heavy-bottomed saucepan.

Place mixture over medium-low heat and beat with an electric mixer constantly for 5-7 minutes, or until fluffy.

Remove from heat and stir in the vanilla. Ice the cooled cake.

KENTUCKY WONDER CAKE

Mix together:

4 eggs
2 cups sugar

Then add:

2 ½ cups flour
1 ½ cups oil
1 ½ tsp. nutmeg
2 ½ tsp. cinnamon
3 ½ tsp, hot water
1 small can crushed pineapple drained
l cup chopped black walnuts

In bowl one, mix eggs, sugar, and hot water.

In second bowl, mix all dry ingredients. Add mixture from bowl one, then mix in pineapple. Blend and then add nuts.

Bake at 350 degrees F, for 1 hour and 15 minutes in a well-greased, floured tube pan.

PINEAPPLE DREAM CAKE

1 box yellow cake mix
1 can (20 ounce) crushed pineapple, well drained
1 pkg. vanilla instant pudding
2 cups milk (to be added to mix)
2 pkg. Dream Whip
1 cup milk (to be added to mix)
1 cup flaked coconut

Using a 9 x 13-inch pan, bake cake as directed on box. Let cool, and spread well drained pineapple on top of cake.

Prepare pudding as directed on box and spread over the pineapple.

Prepare Dream Whip as directed on package and spread over the pudding,

Sprinkle with coconut or chopped pecans.

AUTUMN LEAF CAKE AND GLAZE

1 ½ cups flour (all-purpose)
1 tsp. baking soda
½ tsp. salt
1 tsp. nutmeg
¼ tsp. ginger
¼ tsp. cloves
½ cup margarine or butter
1 cup sugar
1 tsp. vanilla
2 eggs
¾ cup pumpkin

¾ cup chocolate chips
½ cup nuts

Mix all ingredients together.

Bake at 350° F. for 1 hour in loaf pan.

Glaze:

½ cup confectioners' sugar
⅛ tsp. cinnamon
⅛ tsp. nutmeg
1-2 tsp. cream

PUMPKIN CAKE

3 cup sugar
½ tsp. salt
3 ½ cup flour
¼ lb. butter (1 stick)
1 tsp. nutmeg
½ cup nuts
½ cup raisins
1 can pumpkin (1 lb. 13 oz. can)
4 eggs
2 tsp. baking soda
1 cup oil
½ tsp. cloves
1 tsp. cinnamon

Mix dry ingredients together.

Blend softened butter, oil, eggs, into mixture. Blend in raisins and nuts.

Use tube cake pan.

Bake at 350 degrees F. for 1 hour or until done.

BLACKBERRY CAKE AND ICING

2 cups blackberries
1 cup shortening
3 cups self-rising flour
3 eggs
1 tsp. nutmeg
1 tsp. cinnamon
1 tsp. allspice
1 tsp. baking soda
2 cups sugar

Combine all ingredients. Bake at 350 degrees F. until done.

Makes 3 layers.

Icing:

4 cups confectioners' sugar
8 tbsp, butter
6 tbsp. cocoa
8 tbsp. coffee (boiled)
2 tbsp. vanilla

Combine all ingredients. Mix mixture until a spreading consistency forms.

CAJUN CAKE AND EASY COCONUT PECAN ICING

2 cups flour
½ cup sugar
2 tsp. baking soda
2 eggs
1 lb. can crushed pineapple

Mix at medium speed until all ingredients are combined.

Bake in pan (13 x 9 inch).

Preheat oven to 350 degrees F, and bake for 40 to 45 minutes.

Easy Coconut Pecan Icing:

½ cup sugar
½ can evaporated milk
1 stick margarine
1 cup coconut
½ cup chopped nuts (pecans preferred)

Bring sugar and milk to a boil. Add coconut and pecans. Pour over cake.

STRAWBERRY ANGEL FOOD CAKE

1 large angel food cake, baked
2 small or 1 large strawberry Jell-o mix
2 ½ cups boiling water
1 lb. frozen strawberries
1 tbsp. sugar
⅛ tsp. salt
3 pkg. Dream Whip

Dissolve Jell-o in water. Add strawberries and stir until melted. Add sugar and salt. Let this sit in refrigerator just until syrupy.

Prepare 1 package Dream Whip as directed on package and stir into strawberry mixture.

Prepare cake by cubing with a sharp knife on a cutting board.

Layer the cake and strawberry mixture alternately in a 13x9x2 inch pan.

Makes 2 layers. Chill in refrigerator.

Prepare other 2 packages of Dream Whip and ice the whole Cake. Place large fresh strawberries all over it.

FRESH APPLE CAKE

Mix:

1 cup canola oil
2 eggs

Mix and add:

2½ cups. flour
1 tsp. baking soda
1 tsp. baking powder
1 tsp. salt
1 tsp. cinnamon
2 cups sugar
½ cup Angelica
1 cup chopped nuts
3 cups finely chopped apples
1 tsp. vanilla flavoring

Top with one (6-ounce) package butterscotch chips. Bake in 9 x 13-inch pan at 325 degrees for 45 minutes.

Can be served plain or with whipped cream.

FRESH APPLE CAKE (Version 2)

2 cups flour
2 eggs
2 cups sugar
¼ tsp. salt
2 tsp. baking soda
4 cups pared, chopped apples
1 tsp. cinnamon
½ cup chopped walnuts
½ tsp. nutmeg
½ cup soft butter or margarine

Grease 9 x 13-inch pan and preheat oven to 325 degrees.

Sift flour, sugar, baking soda, spices and salt.

Add apples, nuts, butter and eggs. Beat until just combined.

Bake for 1 hour or until top springs back.

Cool on rack.

Serve warm or cold with whipped cream.

7-UP CAKE

1 box (2-layer size) yellow cake mix
1 (3 oz. size) vanilla instant pudding mix
4 eggs
3/4 cup oil

Beat smooth, add:

10 oz. 7-Up

 Blend. Bake at 350 degrees F. for 30 to 35minutes.

Icing:

2 eggs, beaten
1 1/2 cups sugar
1 stick margarine or butter
1 tbsp. flour

Add: 1 cup crushed pineapple (undrained), cook until
thick, add 1 can coconut. Pour over hot cake and serve.

CHOCOLATE SYRUP CAKE

1 stick margarine
1 cup sugar
4 eggs
1 cup cake flour
1 tsp. baking powder
½ tsp. salt
1 can Hershey chocolate syrup

Cream margarine. Add sugar and eggs, one at a time. Sift dry ingredients and add them alternately with chocolate syrup to the creamed mixture.

Bake in a 350 degrees F. oven about 35 minutes, using a 9 x 13-inch pan.

Cool for 10 minutes and cover with warm icing.

Icing:

½ stick margarine or butter
1 cup white sugar
⅓ cup evaporated milk
½ cup chocolate chips

Boil margarine or butter, sugar and milk for 2 minutes. Add chocolate chips and stir until melted. Ice cake immediately. If cake is baked in 2 or 3 layers, double icing recipe.

APRICOT CAKE

Cake:

4 eggs
1/2 cup sugar
3/4 cup oil
1 cup apricot nectar
1 box Lemon Supreme cake mix

Icing:

2 cups powdered sugar
1/4 cups lemon juice
2 tsp. apricot nectar

Beat eggs and sugar. Add oil, apricot nectar and cake mix. Bake in tube pan for 45 minutes at 350 degrees F.

For icing. Mix powdered sugar, lemon juice and apricot nectar and glaze warm cake.

GRAHAM CRACKER CAKE

½ lb. margarine
1 ¼ cups sweet milk
2 cups sugar
1 cup coconut
5 eggs (add 1 at a time)
1 cup nuts, chopped
2 tsp. baking powder
2 tsp. vanilla
1 (16 oz.) box graham cracker crumbs

Mix as for on ordinary coke. Bake in 3 average size layer cake pans at 325 degrees for 45 minutes.

Icing:

Mix together:

1 stick softened margarine or butter.
1 box powdered sugar

Add to sugar mixture:

1 (20 oz.) con crushed pineapple (drained)

Spread icing over cake. Put extra juice in cake.

CHOCOLATE MINT TORTE

4 eggs
1 pkg. (2-layer size) German chocolate cake mix
1 (4 ½ oz.) pkg. instant chocolate pudding
1 cup water
1/3 cup oil
½ cup (½ of 6 oz. pkg.) mint flavored semi-sweet chocolate
2 tsp. oil
2 pkg. dessert topping mix

In large mixer bowl, beat eggs till thick and lemon colored. Blend in cake mix, dry pudding mix, water, and ⅓ cup oil. Beat 4 minutes at medium speed.

Pour into 2 greased and floured 9-inch round layer pans.

Bake in 350 degrees F. oven for 30 minutes or till done.

Cool 10 minutes; remove from pans and cool thoroughly.

Split each layer in half for a total of 4 layers.

Melt together chocolate pieces and 2 teaspoons oil; stir well to combine.

Prepare topping mix according to package directions; set aside 2 cups whipped mixture.

Place one layer on serving plate, spread with half the remaining topping. Place a second layer of cake atop; spread with half the melted chocolate. Repeat layers.

Top layer should have chocolate. Frost sides with the 2. cups reserved topping. Chill 2 to 3 hours.

To serve, let stand at room temperature about 15 minutes.

Makes 16 servings.

WALNUT WONDER CAKE

2 cups flour
1 tsp. baking powder
1 tsp. baking soda
½ tsp. salt
1 cup sugar
2 eggs
1 tsp. vanilla
1 cup margarine or butter
1 cup sour cream
½ cup brown sugar
1 cup sugar
1 tsp. cinnamon
1 cup chopped walnuts

Sift flour, baking powder, baking soda and salt all together.

Cream butter/margarine with 1 cup sugar until light and fluffy. Add eggs and vanilla; beat thoroughly.

Blend by hand sour cream alternately with dry ingredients.

Spread half of batter in greased, floured 9 x 13 x 2-inch pan. Combine remaining ingredients and sprinkle half of mixture over first layer of batter.

Repeat layers and bake in a 350-degree oven for 30 to 35 minutes.

BLUEBERRY CAKE

2 eggs separated
1 cup sugar
¼ tsp. salt
½ cup shortening
1 tsp. vanilla
1 tsp. baking powder
1 ½ cup flour
⅓ cup milk
1 ½ cups fresh blueberries

Beat egg whites until soft peaks form. With same beater, cream shortening with sugar. Beat in egg yolks. Beat well.

Sift dry ingredients together; add alternately with milk. Add vanilla. Fold in beaten egg whites.

Dust blueberries with a tablespoon of flour and stir into batter.

Spread in 8 or 9-inch square cake pan. Sprinkle with a little cinnamon sugar.

Bake 35 to 40 minutes in preheated 350-degree oven until toothpick comes out clean.

RICOTTA CAKE

1 box yellow cake mix
1 ½ lb. Ricotta
1 ½ cups sugar
6 eggs
1½ cups light cream
1 ½ tsp. vanilla
2 tbsp. cinnamon and sugar

Prepare cake mix according to directions.

Pour into large rectangular baking dish.

Mix all other ingredients together (except cinnamon and sugar). Pour over cake batter.

Bake in a 350-degree oven for 1 ½ hours.

Sprinkle cinnamon and sugar (mixed together) on top of cake about 10 minutes before cake is done.

DEATH BY CHOCOLATE

1 box chocolate cake mix
1 cup Kahlua
4 boxes Jell-0 chocolate mousse
2 (12 oz.) tubs whipped topping
6 candy bars like Heath or Symphony Blue

Bake cake according to directions in 9 x 12-inch pan.

Prick cake with fork. Pour Kahlua over cake and soak overnight.

Make the mousse; do not refrigerate.

Cut cake into small cubes.

In a large glass or any see through bowl, press ½ cake cubes.

Follow with ½ chocolate mousse, 2 boxes.

Next layer whipped topping (1 tub); sprinkle with ½ crushed candy (3 bars). Repeat the layering.

Recipe is huge. Enough for about 20 to 30.

POOR MAN'S CAKE

8 tbsp. shortening
1 cup sugar
2 cups flour
1 tsp. cinnamon
½ tsp. nutmeg
½ tsp. allspice
1 tsp. baking soda
1 cup raisins
¾ cup waler

Boil raisins in 2 cups of water. Drain and cool.

Sift all dry ingredients together. Add to sugar, oil and raisins in large mixing bowl. Mix well by hand.

Melt shortening.

Bake in a tube pan in a 350 degrees oven for 50 to 60 minutes.

Sprinkle top with confectioners' sugar.

(This recipe contains no eggs or milk.)

MOUNTAINEER DELIGHT

1 (3-ounce) box lemon pudding mix
1 small angel food cake
½ cup coconut
1 cup crushed pineapple, drained
½ cup chopped pecans
1 (8-ounce) carton frozen, non-dairy whipped topping

Prepare pudding according to box directions; set aside to cool.

Break angel food cake into bite-sized pieces and place in a 13 x 9 x 2-inch baking dish. Cover with lemon pudding. Sprinkle with coconut. Spread pineapple over coconut. Sprinkle with pecans.

Top entire mixture with whipped topping, spreading to the edge of pan to seal.

Refrigerate until serving.

Yield: 12 to 14 servings.

PEACH DELIGHT

1 (19-ounce) can sliced peaches with juice
1 (18½-ounce) box butter pecan cake mix
½ cup butter or margarine
1 (7-ounce) package shredded coconut
1 cup pecans, chopped

Place peaches in the bottom of a 13 x 9 x 2-inch cake pan.

Sprinkle dry cake mix evenly over peaches.

Cut margarine into small squares and place evenly over the cake mix.

Sprinkle with coconut and pecans.

Bake at 350 degrees for 40 minutes.

Serve with whipped topping or ice cream if desired.

Yield: 12 servings.

Pies, Cobblers & Pastry

G.W.'S BLACKBERRY COBBLER

1 stick of butter or margarine
1 cup of sugar
1 cup of flour
¾ cup of milk
2 ½ tsp. baking powder
¾ to 1 cup of blackberries

Preheat your oven to 350 degrees. This cobbler will bake for around 45 minutes.

Melt butter and pour into the bottom of a baking dish.

Mix sugar, flour, milk and baking powder together.

Pour the mix over the butter in your baking dish.

Drop by hand, the blackberries, making sure to evenly distribute them throughout pan.

Bake as indicated above. Let cool before serving.

TENNESSE PEACH PUDDING

2 ½ cups sliced peaches (fresh or frozen)
cooking spray
1 cup all-purpose flour
½ cup granulated sugar
2 tsp. baking powder
½ tsp. salt
½ tsp. ground cinnamon
½ cup milk

Topping:

1 ½ cups water
½ cup granulated sugar
½ cup brown sugar, packed
1 tbsp. butter
¼ tsp. ground nutmeg
2 tbsp. Vanilla Extract

Preheat oven to 400 degrees.

Combine flour, sugar, baking powder, salt and cinnamon.

Stir in milk and vanilla extract until combined.

Fold in peaches. Pour into an oiled 8-inch square baking dish.

For topping, combine water, sugars, butter and nutmeg in a large saucepan. Bring to a boil, stir until sugars are dissolved.

Pour over peach mixture. Bake for 40-50 minutes.

Serve warm or cold.

Top with ice cream to give added flavor.

3 INGREDIENT PEACH COBBLER

32 oz. peaches in heavy syrup 2 (16 ounce) cans, undrained
15 ½ ounces yellow cake mix 1 package
½ cup butter
cinnamon and sugar for top (optional)

Preheat oven to 375 degrees F.

Coat a 9 x 13-inch baking pan with cooking spray.

Empty half of cake mix into bottom of pan.

Empty peaches into pan and mix slightly.

Cover peaches with the rest of cake mix and smooth evenly over the top.

Cut butter into small pieces or melt, and place on top of cake mix.

Sprinkle top with cinnamon and sugar if desired.

Bake for 45 minutes.

BASIC PASTRY RECIPE

7½ cups all-purpose flour, sifted
¼ tsp. salt
2½ cups shortening
1¼ cups ice water

Blend flour and salt in a large mixing bowl.

Cut shortening into dry ingredients with a fork or pastry blender until the size of rice kernels.

Sprinkle water evenly over dry ingredients while tossing it with a fork until all portions are evenly dampened.

Divide into 10 equal portions. Roll each into 9- or 10-inch squares and place on cardboard with a layer of waxed paper between each shell.

Wrap in freezer paper or foil, Freeze until needed,

Yield: 10 (9 inch) pie shells.

COCONUT PIE
(Makes 4)

4 eggs
1 ½ cups sugar
12 tbsp. melted butter
2 cups milk
1 tsp. vanilla
10 oz. coconut dash of salt

Combine all ingredients. Bake at 325 to 350 degrees for about 40 minutes, or until desired brown.

MOTHER'S APPLE PIE

Peel and slice about 5 cups tart apples.

Add to apples:
1 ½ cups sugar
5 tbsp. flour
1 tsp. salt
1 ½ tsp. cinnamon
½ tsp. nutmeg

Mix until apples are well coated.

Use your favorite pie crust and bake 10 minutes at 450 degrees. Reduce heat to 350 degrees and bake for about 45 minutes longer, or until tested done.

SOUR CREAM PIE

1 cup thick sour cream
½ cup sugar
1 cup chopped seeded raisins
3 eggs (using whites of 2 of them for meringue)
1 tsp. allspice
1 tsp. cinnamon

Mix all together and bake in unbaked single crust pie shell.

FRUIT COBBLER 1

½ cup butter or margarine
1 to 1½ quarts berries, cherries or other canned fruit
1 cup sugar
1 cup au-purpose flour
1 cup milk
2 tsp. baking powder

Melt butter or margarine in a flat, 12 x 8 x 2-inch baking pan.

Add fruit to pan.

Mix sugar, flour, milk and baking powder. Spread evenly over fruit. Mixture will be thin.

Bake at 350 degrees for 40 minutes.

Yield: 8 to 10 servings.

CHOCOLATE CHIP WALNUT PIE

3 eggs, slightly beaten
⅛ tsp. salt
1 tsp. vanilla
½ cup sugar
1¼ cups light corn syrup
⅔ cup walnuts
1 cup semi-sweet chocolate morsels
1 (9 inch) pie shell, unbaked

Combine first 5 ingredients. Mix until well blended.

Stir in walnuts and chocolate morsels. Pour mixture into pie shell and bake at 400 degrees for 15 minutes.

Reduce heat to 350 degrees and bake for an additional 35 to 40 minutes or until evenly puffed on top and starting to crack.

Serve warm with whipped cream. Fresh grapes make an attractive garnish for this pie.

Yield: 6 to 8 servings.

Note: This freezes well. To serve after freezing, heat thawed and unwrapped pie at 350 degrees for 15 minutes.

MOMMA G'S COBBLER PIE

1 stick margarine or butter
1 cup sugar
1 cup flour
3/4 cup milk
2 1/2 tsp. baking powder fruit

Melt margarine, in pan. Mix sugar, flour and milk and baking powder. Pour over margarine or butter.

Pour fruit over batter.

Bake at 350 degrees F. for 40 minutes.

COCONUT CUSTARD PIE

1 ½ cup milk
1 ½ tbsp. flour
3 eggs
¼ lb. dry coconut
1 ½ cup sugar
1 tsp. vanilla
1 unbaked pie shell

Beat eggs and sugar until creamy.

Add coconut to flour and mix well.

Add coconut and flour mixture to eggs and sugar.

Add milk and vanilla and stir until well blended.

Pour into pastry lined pie pan and bake at 350 degrees F.
for about 45 minutes.

PECAN PIE

1 cup white corn syrup
1 cup dark brown sugar
⅓ cup melted butter
1 heaping cup pecan halves
4 eggs
vanilla·
salt

Beat eggs until light, add sugar.

Add melted butter, syrup, vanilla and salt and mix well.

Add pecans.

Pour into pie shell and bake at 300 degrees F. approximately 40 minutes.

JELLY ROLL

4 egg yolks
⅓ cup sugar
½ tsp. vanilla
4 egg whites
½ cup sugar
½ cup all-purpose flour
1 tsp. baking powder
¼ tsp. salt
Sifted powdered sugar
½ cup jelly or jam

In small mixing bowl, beat egg yolks at high speed about 5 minutes or until thick and lemon colored.

Gradually add the ⅓ cup sugar, beating until sugar dissolves. Add vanilla; mix well. Wash beaters.

In large mixer bowl beat egg whites at medium speed until soft peaks form. Gradually add the ½ cup sugar; continue beating until stiff peaks form. Fold yolks into whites.

Combine flour, baking powder, and salt; sprinkle over egg mixture. Gently fold in flour mixture until blended.

Grease and flour a 15 x 10 x 1 Jelly roll pan; spread batter evenly in pan.

Bake at 375 degrees for 12 to 15 minutes or until done.

Immediately loosen edges of cake from pan and turn out onto towel and sprinkled with powdered sugar.

Starting with the narrow end, roll the warm cake and towel together; cool on wire rack.

Unroll; spread cake with jelly or jam, leaving a 1 inch rim.

Roll up cake.

Yield: 10 slices.

FRESH APPLE PIE

4 cups apples
2 cups sugar
3 cups flour
2 tsp. soda
2 tsp. cinnamon
1 tsp. salt
2 eggs
1 cup oil
1 cup raisins
½ cup nuts

Preheat oven to 350 degrees F.

Peel and dice apples, then add 2 cups sugar and let stand.

Mix together flour, soda, cinnamon and salt.

Beat eggs and oil and pour into above mixture and mix well.

Add the apples, raisins and nuts.

Bake in tube pan at 300 degrees F. for 1hour.

Icing:
2 cups brown sugar
1 stick butter or margarine
½ cup whole milk

QUICK BANANA BREAD

4 cups biscuit mix
1 cup flour, sifted
1/2 tsp. baking soda
4 eggs, beaten
1 cup sour cream
2 cups mashed very ripe bananas
1 cup chopped nuts

Mix biscuit mix, sugar, flour and soda. Combine eggs and sour cream; stir into dry ingredients with bananas. Stir in nuts. Pour into 2 greased 9x5x3-inch loaf pans.

Bake at 350 degrees for 50 minutes or till it tests done.

Cool 10 minutes in pans; remove from pans and cool on wire racks.

Makes 2 loaves.

CHOCOLATE PIE (9 Inch)

1 cup sugar
3 ½ tbsp. cocoa
⅛ tsp. salt
2 tbsp. cornstarch
3 egg yolks (beaten)
1 tbsp. butter (melted)
1 tsp. vanilla
1 ¼ cups milk

Mix dry ingredients.

Add and mix egg yolks and melted butter.

Add slowly and mix well, vanilla and milk.

Pour into unbaked pie crust.

Bake 10 minutes at 400 degrees and turn heat to 350 degrees for 25 - 30 minutes.

SWEET POTATO PIE

1 ½ cups mashed cooked sweet potato
½ cup sugar
¾ tsp. salt
1 tsp. cinnamon
½ tsp. nutmeg
1 cup milk
2 tbsp. melted butter
2 eggs, separated.
peanuts or pecans may be added if desired (if so - 1/3 cup)
8-inch unbaked pastry shell
6 tbsp. sugar

Combine sweet potato, ½ cup sugar, salt, cinnamon, nutmeg, milk and butter.

Beat egg yolks (add with nuts, if desired).

Pour into pastry shell.

Bake in hot oven (425 F. degrees) 35 minutes or until set.

Optional: Beat egg whites stiff, but not dry. Gradually add remaining sugar, beating constantly. Put through pastry tube on filling. Bake in moderate oven (325 degrees) 20 minutes. Cool.

CHOCOLATE CHESS PIE

Mix these together:

1 cup sugar
3 tbsp. cocoa

Add:

2 beaten eggs
½ stick melted margarine or butter
1 tsp. vanilla
2 tbsp. milk

Bake at 350 degrees for 25 to 30 minutes in unbaked crust.

Start oven at 410 degrees and reduce to 350 degrees when you put pie in oven.

IMPOSSIBLE COCONUT PIE

This pie makes its own crust
(1 recipe makes 2 pies.)

1 ½ cups sugar
½ cup flour
½ tsp. baking powder
4 eggs, well beaten
2 cups milk

¼ cup butter
1 kg. (7 oz.) coconut, flaked
½ tsp. salt tsp.
1 tsp. vanilla

Beat eggs well.

Blend sugar and flour, then add to the eggs.

Add remaining ingredients and MIX THOROUGHLY.

Pour into 2 (9 inch) well-greased pie pans.

Bake at 400 degrees for 35 - 40 minutes or until brown.

Pies will be firm.

COCONUT PIE

2 cups sugar
dash of salt
2 tsp. flour
7 oz. pkg. coconut
1 stick margarine or butter
3 eggs
1 cup sweet milk
2 unbaked pie shells

Melt butter; add sugar and eggs; beat well.

Add additional ingredients and mix well.

Pour in pie shells.

Bake at 350 degrees about 10 minutes until it starts turning brown, then reduce to 325 degrees and bake until set.

BUTTERMILK PIE

⅓ cup melted butter (let cool)
1 ¼ cup white sugar
2 tbsp. all-purpose flour

Combine sugar and flour with the melted butter and mix well.

Add:

2 eggs
1 tsp. vanilla
¼ cup buttermilk

Pour into unbaked 8-inch pie shell.

Bake at 350 degrees for 45 minutes, or until crust is brown.

For a different variety, you can add I small can flaked coconut or a small package of pecans.

APPLE PIE

Pie Crust: (makes 2 crusts)

2 cups flour
1 tsp. salt
⅔ cup butter

Mix flour and salt - take out ⅓ cup and mix with ¼ cup water to form a paste.

Cut butter into remaining flour until the pieces are the size of small peas.

Add flour paste to butter and flour mixture. Mix dough until dough comes together and can be shaped into a ball.

Apple Pie Filling:

6 cups thin sliced apples
1 tsp. flour, if apples are juicy
1 tsp. cinnamon
1 cup sugar

Mix dry ingredients together and combine with apples.

Place in pie crust and dot with 1 ½ tablespoons butter.

Cover with upper crust. Press edges together.

Bake 40 minutes at 425 degrees if using a metal pan or 400 degrees if using a glass pan.

FRESH CHERRY PIE

3 cups pitted sour cherries
1 tbsp. butter
¼ cup flour
1 cup sugar

Mix flour and sugar then toss with cherries to mix well.

Turn into pie shell. Dot with butter. Brush edges of lower crust with water to seal top.

Bake at 425 degrees for 15 minutes and then 350° for 30 minutes.

FRESH PEACH PIE

2 - 2 ½ lbs. peaches
2 tbsp. flour
⅛ tsp. almond extract
¾ cup sugar
2 tbsp. butter

Pare and slice peaches and place in pastry-lined pie pan.

Sprinkle flour and sugar, mixed together, between layers of peaches.

Dot top layer with butter and sprinkle the flavoring over all.

Bake at 425 degrees for 15 minutes, then at 350 degrees for about 20 - 25 minutes.

RHUBARB PIE

5 tbsp. flour
½ tsp. salt beaten egg
2 pie crusts
1 ½ cups sugar
4 cups unpeeled rhubarb in 1-inch pieces

Combine flour, sugar and salt. Toss well with rhubarb.

Heap into pie shell. Dot with butter. Dribble beaten egg over rhubarb.

Cover with top crust.

Bake at 425 degrees for 15 minutes and then 350 degrees for 45 minutes.

PEANUT BUTTER PIE

1 cup powdered sugar
½ cup peanut butter

Mix together.

Use half for the bottom of crust and half over cream filling.

Filling:

¼ cup cornstarch
⅔ cup sugar
¼ tsp. salt
2 cups scalded milk
3 egg yolks, beaten

2 tbsp. butter
1 tsp. vanilla

Cover with meringue or whipped cream.

PUMPKIN PIE

Makes 1 - 9-inch deep-dish pie

1 (9 inch) unbaked deep dish pie crust
¾ cup sugar
1 teaspoon ground cinnamon
½ teaspoon salt
½ teaspoon ground ginger
¼ teaspoon ground cloves
2 eggs

Preheat oven to 425 degrees F.

Combine sugar, salt, cinnamon, ginger and cloves in small
bowl.

Beat eggs lightly in large bowl.

Stir in pumpkin and sugar and spice mixture. Gradually stir
in evaporated milk. Pour into pie shell.

Bake for 15 minutes at 425 degrees. Reduce temperature to
350 degrees F.; bake for 40 to 50 minutes or until knife
inserted near center comes out clean.

Cool on wire rack for 2 hours.

Serve or refrigerate.

Reminder: pumpkin pie needs to be refrigerated.

Cookies & Bars

G.W.'S PEANUT BUTTER COOKIES

½ cup granulated sugar
½ cup packed brown sugar
½ cup peanut butter
¼ cup shortening
¼ cup butter or margarine, softened
1 egg
1 ¼ cups all-purpose flour
¾ tsp. baking soda
½ tsp. baking powder
¼ tsp. salt
Additional sugar to roll cookies in

Mix sugars, peanut butter, shortening, butter and egg in large bowl.

Stir in remaining ingredients. Cover and refrigerate about 2 hours or until firm.

Heat oven to 375°F.

Shape dough into 1 ¼ inch balls. Roll the balls in extra sugar to coat.

Place about 3 inches apart on ungreased cookie sheet. Flatten in crisscross pattern with fork dipped into sugar.

Bake 9 to 10 minutes or until light golden brown.

Cool 5 minutes; remove from cookie sheet. Finish cooling on wire rack.

PUMPKIN COOKIES

1 cup pumpkin
1 cup light raisins
1 cup sugar
1 cup shortening
¼ tsp. salt
1 tsp. vanilla
2 cups flour (all-purpose)
1 tsp. baking soda
1 tsp. baking powder
1 tsp. cinnamon

Combine pumpkin, raisins, sugar, shortening and vanilla.

Sift together remaining ingredients and add to first mixture.

Mix thoroughly. Drop from spoon onto greased cookie sheet.

Bake at 375 degrees about 10 minutes.

G.W.'S CHOCOLATE CHIP PECAN COOKIES

1 ¼ cups all-purpose flour
⅛ tsp. salt
½ cup (1 stick) butter, softened
⅓ cup confectioner's sugar
½ tsp. vanilla extract
½ cup chopped pecans
½ cup milk chocolate chips

In the bowl combine butter and sugar and mix until light and fluffy.

Add to bowl, flour, and salt and mix again.

Add in the vanilla extract, and beat again just until mixed.

Stir in the chocolate chips and pecans and mix until just combined.

Refrigerate for at least 30 minutes before baking.

Use a cookie scoop to make balls and place them on the baking sheet leaving 2 inches between each ball.

Heat oven to 350 degrees F and line 2 baking sheets with parchment paper.

Bake the cookies for 9-11 minutes.

Remove from the oven and leave them on the baking sheet for 5 minutes.

Once cooled, sprinkle with powdered sugar.

PRESSED COOKIES

1 ½ cup butter
1 egg
4 cups sifted all-purpose flour
1 cup sugar
2 tsp. vanilla
1 tsp. baking powder

Thoroughly cream butter and sugar.

Add egg, vanilla; beat well.

Sift together flour and baking powder; add slowly to creamed mixture, mixing to a smooth dough.

Force dough through a cookie press onto ungreased cookie sheet.

Bake in hot oven of 400 degrees for 8 minutes; cool on waxed paper.

Makes 6 dozen.

GRANDMA'S DATE & NUT BARS

1 cup pecans
1 cup chopped dates
2 eggs
2 tsp. maple flavor
1 cup flour, sifted
⅔ cup vegetable oil
1 cup sugar

Mix together your flour and sugar.

Blend together eggs and oil very well and add to your flour and sugar mixture.

Mix together thoroughly, then blend in pecans and dates.

Bake in 325-degree oven for 25 minutes.

APPLE BUTTER DROP COOKIES

½ cup shortening
1 cup brown sugar
1 egg
1 cup apple butter
2 cups flour
½ tsp. baking soda
½ tsp. salt
½ tsp. cinnamon
½ tsp. nutmeg
½ tsp. cloves
½ cup raisins (optional)
¼ cup chopped nuts (optional)

Mix shortening, sugar and egg thoroughly.

Stir in apple butter.

Mix remaining ingredients in apple butter mixture. Chill at least 2 hours.

Bake at 400 degrees for 9 to 12 minutes.

Frost with lemon icing.

CHOCOLATE CHIP COOKIES

⅓ cup shortening, softened
⅓ cup butter or margarine, softened
½ cup sugar
½ cup brown sugar, firmly packed
1 egg
1 tsp vanilla
1½ cups all-purpose flour

½ tsp. baking soda
½ tsp. salt
1 (6-ounce) package semi- sweet chocolate morsels

Cream shortening, margarine, sugar and brown sugar until creamy.

Add eggs and vanilla. Mix until well blended: set aside.

Sift together flour, soda and salt. Add to shortening-egg mixture and mix.

Stir in the chocolate morsels.

Drop by rounded teaspoonful about 2 inches apart on ungreased baking sheet.

Bake at 375 degrees for 8 to 10 minutes or until lightly browned.

Cookies should still be soft. Cool slightly before removing from baking sheet. Cool completely before storing.

Yield: 4 to 5 dozen.

CHOCOLATE MERINGUE COOKIES

2 cups sifted sugar
¾ cup shredded coconut
¼ tsp. salt
1 tbsp. flour
2 or 3 squares unsweetened chocolate, melted & cooled
3 egg whites
1 tsp. vanilla

Sift together sugar, flour and salt.

Beat egg whites until stiff. Add sugar mixture, 2 tablespoons at a time, beating after each addition until blended.

Fold in chocolate, coconut and vanilla.

Drop teaspoon on lightly greased baking sheet. Bake at 375 degrees for about 10 minutes.

Remove from baking sheet immediately.

Cool: store in airtight container.

Makes 2½ dozen 2½-inch cookies.

G.W.'S ULTIMATE CHOCOLATE CHIP COOKIE

¾ cup granulated sugar
¾ cup packed brown sugar
1 cup butter or margarine, softened
1 tsp. vanilla
1 egg
2 ¼ cups all-purpose flour
1 tsp baking soda
½ tsp. salt
1 cup chopped walnuts
1 package milk chocolate chips 12 oz.
¼ cup Belgium chocolate cut into pieces

In a bowl add sugars, softened butter or margarine and mix until fluffy.

Add vanilla extract and egg then mix again.

In a separate bowl add flour, baking soda, salt, and mix together until combined.

Add the flour mix to the first mix. Then add nuts and chocolate to bowl and fold into the mix.

Refrigerate the dough mix for at least 30 minutes.

Preheat oven to 350 degrees before baking.

Use a cookie scoop to place dough on parchment paper lined baking sheets. Leave around 2 inches between cookies.

Bake for at least 11 minutes. Let cool before moving to a cookie rack.

OATMEAL CHOCOLATE CHIP COOKIE BARS

1 cup butter at room temperature
1 cup light brown sugar, packed
½ cup granulated sugar
2 large eggs
2 tsp. vanilla extract
½ tsp. salt
1 tsp. baking soda
1 tsp. baking powder
1 ½ cups all-purpose flour
2 cups old-fashioned rolled oats
2 cups milk chocolate chips

Preheat oven to 350 degrees F.

Lightly grease a 9 x 13-inch pan with cooking spray or line with parchment paper.

In a large mixing bowl beat together the butter, brown sugar, and white sugar until smooth and light.

Add the eggs one at a time, mixing after each addition. Add the vanilla.

In a separate bowl, combine the dry ingredients: salt, baking soda, baking powder, flour and rolled oats.

Add dry ingredients to the creamed mixture and stir until combined.

Add in chocolate chips.

Press into pan and bake for 25 to 30 minutes or until golden brown.

Allow to cool completely before serving.

PECAN SANDIES

1 cup butter
1 tsp. water
2 cups sifted all-purpose flour
⅓ cup sugar
3 tsp. vanilla
1 cup chopped pecans

Cream butter and sugar; add water and vanilla; mix well.

Blend in flour and nuts. Shape into balls and bake on ungreased cookie sheet at 325 degrees about 20 minutes.

Remove from pan; cool slightly; roll in confectioners' sugar.

Makes about 3 dozen.

MOLASSES CRINKLES

¾ cup shortening
1 cup brown sugar
1 egg
4 tbsp. molasses
2 ¼ cups sifted flour
¼ tsp. salt
2 tsp. baking soda
½ tsp. cloves
1 tsp. cinnamon
1 tsp. ginger

Shape into balls the size of walnuts, and dip tops in sugar.

Bake 12 to 15 minutes at 375 degrees.

Makes 3 to 4 dozen cookies.

BROWNIES

2 eggs
½ cup butter
1 tsp. vanilla
¾ cup all-purpose flour
2 squares unsweetened chocolate
1 cup sugar
½ tsp. baking powder
¼ to ½ tsp. salt
¼ cup nuts

Beat eggs 15 minutes or longer.

Melt butter and chocolate in double boiler.

Add sugar to eggs and beat again. Add vanilla. Add chocolate mixture. Add flour, baking powder, salt and nuts.

Bake in a greased and floured 9-inch pan at 350 degrees for 20 minutes. Do not overbake.

Recipe may be doubled and baked on cookie sheet.

Yield: 9 squares.

CHOCOLATE-CARAMEL BARS

1 (18½-ounce) package devil's food cake mix
¾ cup margarine, melted
⅔ cup evaporated milk, divided
1 cup chopped nuts
1 (14-ounce) package light colored caramels
1 (6-ounce) package semi-sweet chocolate morsels

Combine ½ cake mix, butter and ½ cup milk in mixing bowl and mix until well blended.

Stir in nuts. Press 1/2 of this mixture into the bottom of a greased 13 x 9 x 2-inch cake pan.

Bake at 350 degrees for 10 minutes.

While this is baking combine caramels and ⅓ cup milk in the top of a double boiler. Heat over boiling water until caramels melt and mixture is smooth. Pour the caramel mixture over the baked crust.

Sprinkle with chocolate morsels. Top with remaining cake mix. Return to the oven and bake an additional 20 to 25 minutes.

Cool and refrigerate before cutting into bars. Yield: 1 ½ to 2 dozen.

CHOCOLATE-NUT SQUARES

1 cup sugar
5 cups crisp rice cereal
1 cup light corn syrup
2 cups chunky peanut butter
2 tbsp. butter or margarine
1 (12-ounce) package semi-sweet chocolate morsels
½ cup chopped nuts

Combine sugar and syrup in a 3-quart saucepan. Cook over a medium heat, stirring constantly, for 5 minutes or until sugar dissolves.

Remove from heat and blend in peanut butter and margarine. Stir in rice cereal.

Spread peanut butter cereal mixture in a buttered, 12x8x2-inch pan with a tight-fitting cover; set aside.

Place chocolate morsels in a heavy sauce pan or double boiler. Heat over boiling water or a low heat setting, stirring constantly, until morsels are completely melted.

Spread chocolate on cereal mixture. Sprinkle with nuts.

Cover and chill for 1 hour or until topping is firm.

Cut into bars to serve.

Yield: 3 dozen.

TIGER COOKIES

Cream together:

2 sticks margarine or butter (softened)
1 cup sugar

Blend:

2 eggs
1 tsp. vanilla

Add 2 cups self-rising flour. Fold in 3 cups Frosted Flakes (crushed) 1 (10 ounce) box. Swirl in 2 ounces melted chocolate squares.

Bake at 375 degrees for 10 to 12 minutes on ungreased cookie sheet.

Yield: 5 dozen by tablespoon; 7 dozen by teaspoon.

THUMBPRINT COOKIES

⅔ cup butter
⅓ cup granulated sugar
2 egg yolks
1 tsp. vanilla
½ tsp. salt
1 ½ cups flour
2 egg whites
¾ cup walnuts

Cream together butter and sugar till fluffy.

Add egg yolks, vanilla, salt; beat well. Gradually add flour, mixing well.

Shape into 3/4-inch balls; dip in slightly beaten egg whites, then roll in finely chopped walnuts.

Place 1 inch apart on greased cookie sheet. Press down center of each with thumb.

Bake at 350 degrees for 15 to 17 minutes. Cool slightly; remove from pan and cool on rack.

Just before serving, use ⅓ cup cherry, strawberry or mint jelly to fill the centers.

Makes 3 dozen.

LEMON BARS

¼ cup powdered sugar
1 cup sugar
½ cup butter, softened
1 cup all-purpose flour
pinch of salt
2 eggs, beaten
grated rind of 1 lemon
2 tbsp. lemon juice
2 tbsp. all-purpose flour

Cream powdered sugar and butter until light and fluffy; add 1 cup flour and salt, mixing well.

Press mixture into a greased 9-inch square pan.

Bake at 350 degrees for 15 minutes.

Combine remaining ingredients, beating well. Pour over baked crust. Bake at 350 degrees for 20 minutes. Cool; cut into bars.

Yield: 16 bars.

Pudding, Dumplings & Others

RICE PUDDING

1 cup short or medium grain rice, uncooked
3 cups water
2 cups milk
1 tsp. cardamon
Cinnamon for decoration
Syrup or honey, as desired

Wash rice 4 to 5 times with warm water. Change water for each washing.

Combine rice and water in a large saucepan. Bring to a boil over a high heat and cook for 10 minutes, stirring constantly.

Add milk and cardamon.

Decrease heat to low, cover tightly and cook for an additional 55 minutes or until rice is softened completely.

Remove from heat and cool. Pour into serving dishes and decorate with ground cinnamon.

Serve with honey or syrup.

Yield: 12 servings.

INDIAN PUDDING

1 qt. milk
7 tbsp. cornmeal
1 tsp. salt
3/4 cup molasses
1 tbsp. ginger or cinnamon
½ cup cold milk, if desired

Heat 1 quart of milk to boiling point. Add cornmeal and salt and stir well. Add molasses and spices, stirring to blend.

Pour into 1 ½ to 2-quart baking dish and add ½ cup cold milk, if desired.

Bake for 2 hours at 325°.

PUMPKIN PUDDING

6 tbsp. butter
¾ cup brown sugar
½ tsp. salt
½ tsp. baking soda
½ tsp. cinnamon
½ tsp. ginger
¼ tsp. nutmeg
¼ cup granulated sugar
2 eggs
1 ½ cup flour
¾ cup mashed pumpkin
½ cup buttermilk
½ cup chopped walnuts

Cream butter and sugars together until light. Beat in eggs.

Stir together flour, salt, soda, cinnamon, ginger and nutmeg.

Mix pumpkin and buttermilk; add to creamed mixture alternately with dry ingredients. Mix well after each addition.

Fold in nuts.

Spoon into greased and floured 6 1/2-cup ring mold. Cover tightly with foil.

Bake at 350 degrees for 1 hour. Let stand 10 minutes.

Unmold, Serve with whipped cream, if desired.

BAKED APPLES WITH RAISINS

6 medium tart apples
½ cup brown sugar
1 tsp. cinnamon
2 tbsp. butter
½ cup seedless raisins
½ cup water

Wash and core apples. Peel a small portion from the bottom of each.

Mix sugar and cinnamon. Cut butter into sugar mixture.

Stir in raisins. Place apples on rack in the bottom of a heavy skillet.

Fill core of apples as full as possible with sugar mixture.

Pour water in bottom of skillet, crumble remaining sugar mixture over all.

Cover skillet and bake at 350 degrees until apples are tender. Baste often.

Cooking time will vary depending on type of apples used.

APPLE DUMPLINGS

pastry crusts for 10-inch double crust pie
6 whole large apples, peeled and cored
1 ½ cups sugar, divided
¾ tsp. cinnamon, divided
¼ tsp. nutmeg
6 tbsp. butter, divided
2 cups hot water

Preheat oven to 450 degrees 10 minutes before dumplings are ready to be baked.

Roll out pastry ⅛ inch thick and cut it into 6 (7-inch) squares. Place an apple in the center of each square.

Fill apples with a mixture of:

½ cups sugar
½ tsp. cinnamon
¼ tsp. nutmeg
2 tbsp. butter

Moisten edges of pastry with cold water and fold them up around apples, pressing edges together to seal firmly.

Prick pastry in several places. Chill 1 hour.

Combine remaining sugar, cinnamon, butter and 2 cups of hot water. Boil 5 minutes.

Place apples in a 9 x 12-inch baking dish and bake at 450 degrees for 10 minutes.

Reduce heat to 350 degrees. Pour syrup over apples and bake 35 minutes, basting occasionally.

COCONUT RUM BALLS

1 cup finely chopped nuts
4 cups vanilla wafer crumbs
1 (3½-ounce) can flaked coconut
1 (14-ounce) can sweetened condensed milk
¼ cup rum

Combine nuts, wafer crumbs and coconut in mixing bowl. Add milk and rum. Mix until ingredients are well blended.

Chill dough for 4 hours. Shape into walnut-sized balls. Roll in powdered sugar.

Store in container with a tight-fitting lid.

Yield: 2½ to 3 dozen.

Note: These are best made in advance to allow flavor to develop.

QUICK SUGAR DOUGHNUTS

1 can refrigerator buttermilk biscuits
oil for deep frying
1 cup confectioners' sugar

Remove biscuits from can. Flatten a little and push a small hole through center of each.

Fry in hot, deep oil, turning once or twice until golden brown. Drain on paper towel.

Sprinkle with confectioners' sugar.

Serve warm. Makes 10.

POPOVERS

1 cup milk
1 cup flour
4 eggs

Beat eggs slightly; add flour and milk. Do not stir too much.

Bake in hot oven 30 to 40 minutes.

Baked Foods

G.W.'S BAKED MACARONI AND CHEESE

1 ½ cups dry elbow macaroni
3 tbsp. butter or margarine
3 tbsp. all-purpose flour
2 cups milk not skim
½ tsp. each salt and pepper
2 cups shredded cheese (sharp cheddar, Swiss, or
Mozzarella)

Preheat oven to 350 degrees.

Bring a pot of water to a boil; add a sprinkling of salt and
the pasta.

While the pasta cooks, melt the butter in a large skillet.

Add the flour and stir over medium heat until the mix is
lightly browned; 1-2 minutes.

Add the milk and whisk to remove any lumps, then add the
salt and pepper.

Continue to cook until the sauce thickens and bubble.
Around 6 minutes.

Stir in the cheese and whisk until melted. Turn off the heat.

Cook past for ¾ the time recommended, drain and add to
the sauce.

Stir the pasta into the sauce.

Bake in a greased 2-quart dish for 20-25 minutes, until
browned and bubbling.

CHICKEN LOAF

(4-pounds) chicken, bolled, boned and cut into bite-sized
chunks, or 3 cups chopped chicken
2 cups breadcrumbs
1 cup cooked rice
1 (2-ounce) jar pimentos, finely chopped
1 ½ cups chicken broth
1 ½ cups milk
3 or 4 eggs, well beaten
Salt, to taste
Pepper, to taste
Paprika

Combine ingredients in bowl and mix until well blended.

Pour into a buttered, 9 x 5 x 3-inch, loaf pan. Sprinkle with
paprika.

Carefully place loaf pan in a 13 x 9 x 2-inch pan containing
½ inch hot water.

Bake at 350 degrees for 1 ½ hours.

Serve with Hot Mushroom Sauce or gravy.

Yield: 6 to 8 servings.

OVEN BARBECUED CHICKEN

1 (3-pound) fryer
Salt and pepper to taste
½ cup melted butler
1 tbsp. lemon juice
2 tbsp. paprika
½ cup salad dressing
½ cup hot catsup
2 tbsp. honey

Cut chicken into serving-sized pieces and season.

Combine remaining ingredients in a 13 x 9 x 2-inch baking pan.

Arrange chicken in a single layer. Turn once to coat with butter mixture.

Bake at 350 degrees for 45 to 60 minutes or until done.

Baste every 15 minutes while baking. Yield: 4 to 6 servings.

DRUNKEN CHICKEN

1 (10 ¾ -ounce) can cream of celery soup
1 (10 ¾ -ounce) can cream of mushroom soup
1 cup rice, uncooked
1 cup cooking sherry
1 (2½ to 3-pound) frying chicken, cut up
1 (1 ⅜ -ounce) envelope instant onion soup

Combine first 4 ingredients and mix until well blended.

Place in a greased, 13 x 9 x 2 inch, baking pan. Top with chicken parts (preferably skinless). Sprinkle with onion soup mix.

Cover tightly with foil, Bake at 350 degrees for 2 hours. Yield: 4 servings,

Note: If desired, rice can be eliminated from ingredients and chicken served over noodles.

CHICKEN DIVAN

2 (10-ounce) packages frozen broccoli spears
1 cup cubed, cooked chicken
½ cup mayonnaise
1 (10½-ounce) can cream of chicken soup
1 tbsp. lemon juice
½ cup sour cream
½ tsp. curry
1 cup shredded Cheddar cheese
½ cup cracker crumbs
Slivered almonds

Place broccoli in a greased, 12 x 8 x 2 inch, microwave safe dish. Cover with plastic wrap. Microwave on high for 10 minutes, then drain.

Place chicken over broccoli.

Blend mayonnaise, chicken soup, lemon juice, sour cream and curry. Stir in cheese. Pour over chicken, Sprinkle with cracker crumbs and almonds.

Cover and bake in over at 350 degrees for 25 minutes.
Yield: 6 servings.

CHICKEN RICE CASSEROLE

(2½ to 3-pound) fryer, cut into serving pieces
2 cups long grain rice, un- cooked
1 (1 ⅜ -ounce) package onion soup mix
1 (10 ½ -ounce) can cream of chicken soup
1 (10 ¾ -ounce) can cream of mushroom soup
3 (10 ¾ -ounce) cans water

Place rice in the bottom of a greased, 13 x 9 x 2-inch
baking dish. Place chicken on rice.

Combine soups and water; mix until well blended. Pour
soup mixture over chicken.

Bake uncovered, at 350 degrees for 1½ hours.

Yield: 6 to 8 servings.

CHICKEN SPAGHETTI CASSEROLE

2½ cups uncooked spaghetti, broken
3 to 4 cups diced boiled chicken
½ cup pimento
1 small onion, chopped
1 tsp. salt
2 (10 ¾ -ounce) cans cream of mushroom soup
1 (10 ¾ -ounce) can chicken broth or cream of chicken
soup

Pepper to taste
3 cups grated sharp Cheddar cheese

Combine all ingredients except cheese in a mixing bowl and mix until well blended.

Pour into a greased. 2-quart casserole dish. Cover with cheese. refrigerate overnight.

Bake, uncovered, at 300 degrees for 45 minutes to 1 hour.

Yield: 6 to 8 servings.

SAUSAGE BREAKFAST CASSEROLE

12 slices extra thin white bread
butter
1½ pounds sausage
1 pound shredded sharp Cheddar cheese
4 eggs, beaten
3 cups milk

Trim crust from bread slices and lightly butter.

Place 6 slices of bread, buttered side up, in a well buttered. 13 x 9 x 2-inch, baking dish.

Sauté sausage over medium-high heat until browned. Spread ½ sausage over bread.

Top with layer of ½ of the cheese. Repeat layers with remaining bread, sausage and cheese.

Combine eggs and milk. Pour over casserole.

Press down until milk seeps through bread. Cover and refrigerate overnight.

Bake at 350 degrees for 1 hour. Yield: 6 servings.

STUFFED SHELLS

24 jumbo macaroni shells
1 (13-ounee) jar spaghetti sauce with mushrooms
1 (10-ounce) package frozen chopped broccoli or spinach, thawed and drained
2 cups ricotta cheese
2 cups shredded mozzarella cheese
1 small onion. diced
½ cup grated Parmesan cheese
2 tbsp. chopped fresh parsley
1 tsp. dried whole oregano
⅛ tsp. ground nutmeg
⅛ tsp. hot sauce
¼ cup Parmesan cheese

Cook macaroni shells according to package directions; drain.

Spoon 1 cup spaghetti sauce into a lightly greased 13 x 9 x 2-inch baking dish.

Set aside remaining sauce.

Combine next 9 ingredients and mix until well blended.

Stuff each shell with 1 ½ tablespoons of mixture and place in baking dish.

Spoon remaining sauce over shells.

Sprinkle with l6 cup Parmesan cheese.

Cover and bake at 350 degrees for 30 to 40 minutes.

Yield: 6 to 8 servings.

QUICK 'N CHEESY MACARONI AND BROCCOLI

1 (10-ounce) box chopped broccoli with cheese sauce
½ cup uncooked elbow macaroni
2 tbsp. sliced green onions
2 tbsp. mayonnaise
2 tsp. lemon juice
1 small tomato, peeled and cut into wedges
2 tbsp. grated Parmesan cheese·

Cook broccoli according to package directions.

Cook macaroni, drain, and put into 1 quart casserole dish.

Stir in onions, mayonnaise, lemon juice and broccoli.

Garnish with tomato wedges and sprinkle with cheese.

Broil 3 to 5 minutes at 350 degrees.

Yield: 2 servings.

BROCCOLI CASSEROLE

2 (10-ounce) packages frozen broccoli spears
¼ cup butter
1 medium-sized onion, chopped
1 (10¾-ounce) can cream of mushroom soup
4 slices cheese
Sprinkle of garlic
Seasoned croutons

Cook broccoli in boiling water just until tender: drain.

Melt butter in small skillet. Add onion and sauté over a medium-high heat until onions ae transparent.

Place broccoli in a buttered, 2-quart casserole dish. Cover with sauteed onions and butter. Add mushroom soup.

Place cheese slices over mixture. Sprinkle with garlic and top with croutons.

Bake at 300 degrees for 30 minutes.

Yield: 4 to 6 servings.

BROCCOLI CHEESE CASSEROLE

1 large bunch fresh broccoli, chopped
2 cups uncooked quick cooking rice
½ cup chopped onion
1 (10 ounce) can cream of celery soup
1 (10 ¾-ounce) can cream of mushroom soup
I (8-ounce) jar processed cheese spread
½ cup melted butter

Combine ingredients in a large mixing bowl and mix until well blended.

Pour into a greased. 2-quart casserole. Bake, covered at 350 degrees for 30 minutes. Uncover and bake an additional 30 minutes.

Yield: 20 servings.

BAKED BEANS

2 cans pork and beans (15 oz. sizes)
grated cheese (about 1/2 cup)
5 slices bacon, cut in small pieces
1 small onion
1 small green pepper (if desired)
1 cup barbecue sauce
1/2 cup water

Mix together all the above ingredients.

Put into 2-quart casserole dish and bake in oven at 350 degrees F. for 35 minutes or until onions are done.

CORN PUDDING

2 cup stewed corn
2 cups milk
3 eggs
1 tbsp. butter
1 tbsp. minced onion
2 tbsp. sugar
¼ cup minced green pepper
1 minced pimiento
1 tsp. salt

Beat eggs slightly.

Add milk, sugar, and salt.

Combine corn with other ingredients and add to the milk mixture. Mix well.

Turn into a buttered casserole and bake in moderate oven (325 degrees F,) for 1 hour.

Serve hot with cheese or tomato sauce.

Serves 6

FRENCH BAKED POTATOES

Peel medium potatoes and roll each potato in melted butter or margarine. Then roll each potato in cracker meal or bread crumbs. Salt and pepper.

Place potatoes in pan with cover and let bake at 375 degrees until potatoes are tender.

Remove cover and bake until potatoes have a slight crust on outside.

LEFTOVER TURKEY CASSEROLE RECIPE

6 cups cooked turkey (cut into medium pieces)
4 cups bread stuffing
2 cans cream of chicken soup
1 cup milk

Preheat your oven to 350°F.

Spray the bottom of a 9×13 baking dish with non-stick cooking spray.

Cover the bottom of the baking dish with the cooked turkey.

Crumble the dressing over the top of the turkey.

Mix the canned soup with the milk and pour over the dressing and turkey.

Bake until bubbling, around 40 to 50 minutes.

CORNBREAD STUFFING

8 tablespoons (1 stick) unsalted butter
1 cup chopped yellow onion
5 cups cubed cornbread, (recipes are in this book)
2 teaspoons chopped sage leaves
2 ribs celery, diced
2 tablespoons poultry seasoning
½ cup chicken stock
2 tablespoons parsley leaves
2 teaspoons salt
½ teaspoon ground black pepper

Preheat oven to 400 degrees F.

Melt the butter in a medium sized pot. Add onions and cook for 5 minutes over medium heat, until the onions are translucent.

Put the cornbread cubes in a large bowl. Add the cooked onions, sage, celery, poultry seasoning, chicken stock, parsley, salt and pepper, and mix thoroughly.

Place in a greased baking dish and bake at 400 degrees for 15 minutes, until golden-brown.

BEEF POT ROAST

3-4 lb. chuck roast
1 tsp. black pepper
1 tsp. powdered garlic
1 tsp. salt
2 tsp. beef base (bouillon cubes or Better Than Bouillon)
2 tsp. olive oil
1 tbsp. Worcestershire Sauce
1 large yellow onion (diced)
2 celery ribs (sliced)
4-5 garlic cloves (sliced)
Cornstarch Slurry (2 tsp each of cornstarch and water mixed together)

Season the chuck roast on both sides with salt, pepper and powdered garlic.

In a large skillet over medium high heat, add the olive oil and brown the roast on both sides.

Add the remaining ingredients except the cornstarch slurry and mix well.

Bring to a boil, reduce the heat to medium low, cover and let braise 3-4 hours until fork tender.

Then remove the roast and remaining solid ingredients.

Bring back to a light boil and add corn starch slurry. Mix well until thickened, about 1 minute.

Return roast and other ingredients to pan with sauce.

Helpful Hints

Abbreviations Commonly Used

tsp. • teaspoon
tbsp. • tablespoon
c. • cup
pt. • pint
qt. • quart
pk. • peck
bu. • bushel
oz. • ounce or ounces
lb. • pound or pounds
sq. • square
min. • minute or minutes
hr. • hour or hours
mod. • moderate or moderately
doz. • dozen

Oven Temperatures

Slow	250 to 300 Degrees
Slow moderate	325
Moderate	350
Quick moderate	375
Moderately hot	400
Hot	425 to 450
Very Hot	475 to 500

Contents Of Cans

Of the different sizes of cans used by commercial canners, the most common are:

Size	Average contents
8 oz.	1 cup
picnic	1 1/4 cups
#300	1 3/4 cups
No. 1 tall	2 cups
No. 303	2 cups
No. 2	2 1/2 cups
No. 2 1/2	3 1/2 cups
No. 3	4 cups
No. 10	12 to 13 cups

How to Avoid Food Poisoning
In Home-Cooked Foods

Proper cooking and handling of food can reduce the risk of food poisoning. Salmonella and other bacteria can be present in meat and poultry products without giving off any telltale signs, like bad taste or bad smell, so it's important to prevent these bacteria from spreading or multiplying to dangerous levels. The basic rule is: keep hot foods hot and cold foods cold. Here are some recommendations for avoiding trouble:

- Don't thaw meat or poultry on the kitchen counter. Instead, thaw it overnight in the refrigerator, or put frozen package in a watertight plastic bag under cold water, changing the water often.

- Don't leave hot food out for more than two hours. Even in a chafing dish, the food often isn't kept hot enough to discourage bacteria growth.

- Don't cool leftovers on the kitchen counter. It's safer to put them straight into the refrigerator.

- Pick up perishable foods last when grocery shopping, and get them home and into the refrigerator quickly.

- Repeated handling can introduce bacteria into food. Leave food in the original store wrapper when refrigerating.

- Keep your refrigerator set at 40 degrees or lower.

Cook meat and poultry thoroughly to kill bacteria. Most food poisoning bacteria are killed at cooking temperatures between 165 degrees and 212 degrees. Use a meat thermometer, instead into the thickest part, away from the bone or fat.

Freeze Now – Heat Later

One of the best things about modern times that the good old days lacked is refrigeration, and the convenience of cooking food ahead of time, freezing it, and then being able to just heat it up when we need it. Here are some tips on using your freezer to keep foods tasting delicious and staying fresh:

- Always chill dishes freezing them, since a still-warm dish takes longer to freeze and allows the formation of ice crystals that change the color, taste, and texture of the food.

- Ceramic, metal, or glass baking dishes may be used to freeze prepared foods if they are tightly covered. Use packaging materials that are moisture proof, reasonably airtight, and durable. Heavy aluminum foil, freezer paper or bags, poly wrap, and strong plastic containers protect foods from freezer burn.

- Leave about half an inch of space (especially for foods with a sauce) so foods will have room to expand while freezing. When storing food in bags, press out excess air before sealing.

- Before you freeze, label each package with the contents, date prepared, and the number of servings.

- Don't freeze emulsified sauces such as hollandaise sauce; they will curdle and separate. Cream sauces are also risky to freeze, and gelatin or whipped-cream desserts don't freeze successfully.

- Be sure that your freezer is cold enough. Frozen foods held at 0 degrees or lower retain their quality longer.

Suggested Maximum Home-Storage Periods to Maintain Good Quality in Purchased Frozen Foods

Food	Approximate holding period at 0 degrees Fahrenheit

Fruits and Vegetables

	Months
Fruits, fruit juice concentrates	12
Vegetables	8

Baked Goods

Bread and yeast rolls:	
White Bread	3
Cinnamon Rolls	2
Plain Rolls	3
Cakes:	
Chocolate layer	4
Pound or Yellow	6
Fruit	12
Pies (unbaked):	
Apple and other fruit	8

Meat

Beef:	
Hamburger	4
Roasts and Steaks	12
Lamb:	
Patties (ground meat)	4
Roasts	9
Pork, cured:	2
Pork, fresh:	
Chops	4
Roasts	8
Veal:	
Cutlets, chops, and roasts	9
Cooked meat:	
Meat dinners and pies	3

Suggested Maximum Home-Storage Periods to Maintain Good Quality in Purchased Frozen Foods

Food	Approximate holding period at 0 degrees Fahrenheit

Poultry

	Months
Chicken:	
Cut-up	9
Whole	12
Duck or goose, whole:	6
Turkey:	
Cut-up	6
Whole	12
Cooked chicken or turkey dinners:	6

Fish and Shellfish

Fish Fillets:	
Cod, Flounder, Haddock, Halibut, Pollack	6
Mullet, Ocean Perch, Sea Trout, Striped Bass	3
Salmon steaks	2
Whiting, drawn	4
Shellfish:	
Clams, shucked	3
Oysters, shucked	4
Crabmeat:	
Dungeness	3
King	10
Shrimp:	12
Cooked fish and shellfish:	3

Frozen Desserts

Ice Cream or Sherbet	1

Cooking Tips

1. After stewing a chicken, cool in broth before cutting into chunks; it will have twice the flavor.
2. To slice meat into thin strips, as for stir-fry dishes, partially freeze it so it will slice more easily.
3. A roast with the bone in it will cook faster than a boneless roast. The bone carries the heat to the inside more quickly
4. When making a roast, place a dry onion soup mix in the bottom of your roaster pan. After removing the roast, add 1 can of mushroom soup and you will have good brown gravy.
5. For a juicier hamburger, add cold water to the beef before grilling (1/2 cup to 1 lb. of meat).
6. To freeze meatballs, place them on a cookie sheet until frozen. Place in plastic bags. They will stay separated so that you may remove as many as you want.
7. To keep cauliflower white while cooking, add a little milk to the water.
8. When boiling corn, add sugar to the water instead of salt. Salt will toughen the corn.
9. To ripen tomatoes, put them in a brown paper bag in a dark pantry, and they will ripen overnight.
10. To keep celery crisp, stand it upright in a pitcher of cold, salted water and refrigerate.
11. When cooking cabbage, place a small tin cup or a can half full of vinegar on stove near the cabbage. It will absorb the odor.
12. Potatoes soaked in salt water for 20 minutes before baking will bake more rapidly.
13. Let raw potatoes stand in cold water for at least a half-hour before frying in order to improve the crispness of French-fried potatoes. Dry potatoes thoroughly before adding to oil.

14. Use greased muffin tins as molds when baking stuffed green peppers.
15. A few drops of lemon juice in water will whiten boiled potatoes.
16. Buy mushrooms before they "open". When stems and caps are attached firmly, mushrooms are truly fresh.
17. Do not use metal bowls when mixing salads. Use wood, glass, or china.
18. Lettuce keeps better if you store it in the refrigerator without washing it. Keep the leaves dry. Wash lettuce the day you are going to use it.
19. Do not use baking soda to keep vegetables green. It destroys Vitamin C.
20. Do not despair if you over-salt gravy. Stir in some instant mashed potatoes to repair the damage. Just add a little more liquid in order to offset the thickening.
21. A leaf of lettuce dropped into the pot absorbs the grease from the top of soup.   Remove the lettuce and throw it away as soon as it has served its purpose.
22. To prevent splashing when frying meat, sprinkle a little salt into the pan before putting in the fat.
23. When bread is baking, a small dish of water in the oven will help to keep the crust from getting hard.
24. Rinse a pan in cold water before scalding milk to prevent sticking.
25. When you are creaming butter and sugar together, it's a good idea to rinse the bowl with boiling water first. They'll cream faster.
26. Dip the spoon in hot water to measure shortening, butter, etc.; the fat will slip out more easily.
27. Using a can opener that leaves a smooth edge, remove both ends from a flat can (the size that tuna is usually packed in) and you have a perfect mold for poaching eggs.
28. When preparing to bake biscuits, use the divider from an ice tray. Shape the dough to conform to the size of

the try, and press divider on dough. After baking the biscuits will separate at dividing lines.

29. Try using a thread instead of a knife when a cake is to be cut while it is still hot.
30. For lump-less gravies and creamy smooth sauces, use a small spring whisk and stir till all ingredients are blended.

Herbs & Spices

Acquaint yourself with herbs and spices. Add in small amounts, ¼ tsp. for every 4 servings. Crush dried herbs or snip fresh ones before using. Use 3 times more fresh herbs if substituting fresh for dried.

Basil – Sweet, warm flavor with an aromatic odor. Use whole or ground. Good with lamb, roast, stews, ground beef, vegetables, dressing and omelets.

Bay Leaves – Pungent flavor. Use whole leaf but remove before serving. Good in vegetable dishes, seafood, stews and pickles.

Caraway – Spicy taste and aromatic smell. Use in cakes, breads, soups, cheese and sauerkraut.

Chives – Sweet, mild flavor like that of onion. Excellent in salads, fish, soups and potatoes.

Cilantro – Use fresh. Excellent in salads, fish, chicken, rice, beans and Mexican dishes.

Curry Powder – Spices are combined to proper proportions to give a distinct flavor to meat, poultry, fish, and vegetables.

Dill – Both the seeds and leaves are flavorful. Leaves may be used as garnish or cooked with fish, soup, dressings, potatoes, and beans. Leaves or the whole plant may be used to flavor pickles.

Fennel – Sweet, hot flavor. Both the seeds and leaves are used. Use in small quantities in pies and baked goods. Leaves can be boiled with fish.

Ginger – A pungent root, this aromatic spice is sold fresh, dried or ground. Use in pickles, preserves, cakes, cookies, soups, and meat dishes.

Marjoram – May be used either dried or green. Use to flavor fish, poultry, omelets, lamb, stew, stuffing, and tomato juice.

Mint – Aromatic with a cool flavor. Excellent in beverages, fish, lamb, cheese, soup, peas, carrots, and fruit desserts.

Oregano – Strong, aromatic odor. Use whole or ground in tomato juice, fish, eggs, pizza, omelets, chili, stew, gravy, poultry, and vegetables.

Paprika – A bright red pepper, this spice is used in meat, vegetables, and soups or as a garnish for potatoes, salads, or eggs.

Parsley – Best when used fresh, but it can be used dried as a garnish or as a seasoning. Try in fish, omelets, soup, meat, stuffing, and mixed greens.

Rosemary – Very aromatic. It can be used either fresh or dried. It can be used to season fish, stuffing, beef, lamb, poultry, onions, eggs, bread, and potatoes. Great in dressings.

Saffron – Orange-yellow in color, this spice flavors or colors foods. Use in soup, chicken, rice, and breads.

Sage – Use either fresh or dried. The flowers are sometimes used in salads. May be used in tomato juice, fish, omelets, beef, poultry, stuffing, cheese spreads and breads.

Tarragon – Leaves have a pungent, hot taste. Use to flavor sauces, salads, fish, poultry, tomatoes, eggs, green beans, carrots, and dressings.

Thyme – Sprinkle leaves on fish or poultry before broiling or baking. Throw a few sprigs directly on coals shortly before meat is finished grilling.

Baking Breads
Hints for Baking Breads

1. Kneading the dough for 30 seconds after mixing improves the texture of baking powder biscuits.
2. Instead of shortening, use cooking or salad oil in waffles and hot cakes
3. When bread is baking, a small dish of water in the oven will help keep the crust from hardening.
4. Dip a spoon in hot water to measure shortening, butter, etc., and the fat will slip out more easily.
5. Small amounts of leftover corn may be added to pancake batter for variety.
6. To make bread crumbs, use the fine cutter of a food grinder and tie a large paper bag over the spout in order to prevent flying crumbs.
7. When you are doing any sort of baking you get better results if you remember to preheat your cookie sheet, muffin tins or cake pan.

Rules for Use of Leavening Agents

1. In simple flour mixtures, use 2 tsp. baking powder to leaven 1 cup flour. Reduce this amount by ½ tsp. for each egg used.
2. To 1 tsp. baking soda use 2 ¼ tsp. cream tarter, 2 cups freshly soured milk, or 1 cup molasses.
3. To substitute baking soda and an acid for baking powder, divide the amount of baking powder by 4. Take that as your measure and add acid according to rule 2.

Proportions of Baking Powder to Flour

Biscuits...	To 1 cup flour use 1 ¼ tsp. baking powder
Cake with oil.....................................	To 1 cup flour use 1 tsp. baking powder
Muffins...	To 1 cup flour use 1 ½ tsp. baking powder
Popovers...	To 1 cup flour use 1 ¼ tsp. baking powder
Waffles...	To 1 cup flour use 1 ¼ tsp. baking powder

Proportions of Liquid to Flour

Drop Batter....................................	To 1 cup liquid use 2 to 2 ½ cups flour
Pour Batter....................................	To 1 cup liquid use 1 cup flour
Soft Dough....................................	To 1 cup liquid use 3 to 3 ½ cups flour
Stiff Dough....................................	To 1 cup liquid use 4 cups flour

Baking Breads
Time and Temperature Chart

Breads	Minutes	Temperature (degrees)
Biscuits...... ...	12-15	.......................400 – 450
Cornbread... ...	25-30	.......................400 – 425
Gingerbread	40-50	.......................350 – 370
Loaf............ .	50-60	.......................350 – 400
Nut Bread......	50-75	350
Popovers...... .	30-40	.......................425 – 450
Rolls......... ...	20-30	.......................400 - 450

Baking Desserts
Perfect Cookies

Cookie dough that is to be rolled is much easier to handle after it has been refrigerated for 10 to 30 minutes. This keeps the dough from sticking, even though it may be soft. If not done, the soft dough may require more flour and too much flour makes cookies hard and brittle. Place on a floured board only as much dough as can be easily managed. Flour the rolling pin slightly and roll lightly to desired thickness. Cut shapes close together and add trimmings to the dough that needs to be rolled. Place pans or sheets in upper third of oven. Watch the cookies carefully while baking in order to avoid burned edges. When sprinkling sugar on cookies, try putting it into a salt shaker in order to save time.

Perfect Pies

1. Pie crust will be better and easier to make if all the ingredients are cool.
2. The lower crust should be placed in the pan so that it covers the surface smoothly. Air pockets beneath the surface will push the crust out of shape while baking.
3. Folding the top crust over the lower crust before crimping will keep juices in the pie.
4. In making custard pie, bake at a high temperature for about 10 minutes to prevent a soggy crust. Then finish baking at a low temperature.
5. When making cream pie, sprinkle crust with powdered sugar in order to prevent it from becoming soggy.

Perfect Cakes

1. Fill cake pans 2/3 full and spread batter into the corners and sides, leaving a slight hollow in the center.
2. Cake is done when it shrinks from the sides of the pan or if it springs back when touched lightly with the finger.
3. After removing a cake from the oven, place it on a rack for about 5 minutes. Then, the sides should be loosened and the cake turned out a rack in order to finish cooling.
4. Do not frost cakes until thoroughly cool.
5. Icing will remain where you put it if you sprinkle cake with powdered sugar first.

Baking Desserts
Time and Temperature Chart

Dessert	Time	Temperature (degrees)
Butter cake, layer....	20-40 min.	...........380 – 400
Butter cake, loaf......	40-60 min.	...........360 – 400
Cake, angel............	50-60 min.	...........300 – 360
Cake, fruit............	3-4 hrs.	...........275 – 325
Cake, sponge.........	40-60 min.	...........300 – 350
Cookies, molasses...	18-20 min.	...........350 – 375
Cookies, thin.........	10-12 min.	...........380 – 390
Cream Puffs...........	45-60 min.	...........300 – 350
Meringue..............	40-60 min.	...........250 – 300
Pie Crust..............	20-40 min.	...........400 - 500

Vegetables & Fruits

Vegetables	Cooking Method	Time
Artichokes	boiled	40 min.
	steamed	45 – 60 min.
Asparagus, tips	boiled	10 -15 min.
Beans, lima	boiled	20 – 40 min.
	steamed	60 min.
Beans, string	boiled	15 -35 min.
	steamed	60 min.
Beets, old	boiled or steamed	1 – 2 hrs.
Beets, young with skin	boiled	30 min.
	steamed	60 min.
	baked	70 – 90 min.
Broccoli, flowerets	boiled	5 – 10 min.
Broccoli, stems	boiled	20 – 30 min.
Brussels, sprouts	boiled	20 – 30 min.
Cabbage, chopped	boiled	10 – 20 min.
	steamed	25 min.
Carrots, cut across	boiled	8 – 10 min.
	steamed	40 min.
Cauliflower, flowerets	boiled	8 – 10 min.
Cauliflower, stem down	boiled	20 – 30 min.
Corn, green, tender	boiled	5 – 10 min.
	steamed	15 min.
	baked	20 min.
Corn on the cob	boiled	8 – 10 min.
	steamed	15 min.
Eggplant, whole	boiled	30 min.
	steamed	40 min.
	baked	45 min.

Parsnips	boiled	25 – 40 min.
	steamed	60 min.
	baked	60 – 75 min.
Peas, green	boiled or steamed	5 – 15 min.
Potatoes	boiled	20 – 40 min.
	steamed	60 min.
	baked	60 – 75 min.
Pumpkin or Squash	boiled	20 – 40 min.
	steamed	45 min.
	baked	60 min.
Tomatoes	boiled	5 – 15 min.
Turnips	boiled	25 – 40 min.

Vegetables & Fruits
Drying Time Table

Fruits	Sugar or Honey	Cooking Time
Apricots..................	¼ cup for each cup of fruit	.............About 40 min.
Figs..................….....	1 tablespoon for each cup of fruit	.............About 30 min.
Peaches..................	¼ cup for each cup fruit	.............About 45 min.
Prunes.................…...	2 T. for each cup of fruit	.............About 45 min.

Buying Fresh Vegetables

Artichokes: Look for compact, tightly closed heads with green, clean-looking leaves. Avoid those with leaves that are brown or separated.

Asparagus: Stalks should be tender and firm; tips should be close and compact. Choose the stalks with very little white; they are more tender. Use asparagus soon because it toughens rapidly.

Beans, Snap: Those with small seeds inside the pods are best. Avoid beans with dry-looking pods.

Broccoli, Brussels Sprouts, and Cauliflower: Flower clusters on broccoli and cauliflower should be tight and close together. Brussels sprouts should be firm and compact. Smudgy, dirty spots may indicate pests or disease.

Cabbage and Head Lettuce: Choose heads that are heavy for their size. Avoid cabbage with worm holes and lettuce with discoloration or soft rot.

Cucumbers: Choose long, slender cucumbers for best quality. May be dark or medium green, but yellow ones are undesirable.

Mushrooms: Caps should be closed around the stems. Avoid black or brown gills.

Peas and Lima Beans: Select pods that are well-filled but not bulging. Avoid dried, spotted, yellow, or flabby pods.

Buying Fresh Fruits

Bananas: Skin should be free of bruises and black or brown spots. Purchase them green and allow them to ripen at home at room temperature.

Berries: Select plump, solid berries with good color. Avoid stained containers which indicate wet or leaky berries. Berries with clinging caps, such as blackberries and raspberries, may be unripe. Strawberries without caps may be overripe.

Melons: In cantaloupes, thick, close netting on the rind indicates best quality. Cantaloupes are ripe when the stem scar is smooth and the space between the netting is yellow or yellow-green. They are best when fully ripe with fruity odor.

Honeydews are ripe when the rind has a creamy to yellowish color and velvety texture. Immature honeydews are whitish-green.

Ripe watermelons have some yellow color on one side. If melons are white or pale green on one side, they are not ripe.

Oranges, Grapefruit, and Lemons: Choose those heavy for their size. Smoother, thinner skins usually indicate more juice. Most skin markings do not affect quality. Oranges with a slight greenish tinge may be just as ripe as fully colored ones. Light or greenish-yellow lemons are more tart than deep yellow ones. Avoid citrus fruits showing withered, sunken or soft areas.

Measurements & Substitutions

Measurements

A pinch	1/8 tsp. or less
3 tbsp.	1 tablespoon
4 tbsp.	¼ cup
8 tbsp.	½ cup
12 tbsp.	¾ cup
16 tbsp.	1 cup
2 cups	1 pint
4 cups	1 quart
4 quarts	1 gallon
8 quarts	1 peck
4 pecks	1 bushel
16 ounces	1 pound
32 ounces	1 quart
1 ounce liquid	2 tbsp.
8 ounce liquid	1 cup

**Use standard measuring spoons and cups.
All measurements are level.**

Substitutions

Ingredient	Quantity	Substitute
Baking Powder	1 tsp.	¼ tsp. baking soda plus ½ tsp. cream of tarter
Ketchup or Chili Sauce	1 cup	1 cup tomato sauce plus ½ cup sugar and 2 tbsp. vinegar (for use in cooking)
Chocolate	1 square (1oz.)	3 or 4 tbsp. plus 1 tbsp. butter
Cornstarch	1 tbsp	2 tbsp. four or 2 tsp. quick tapioca
Cracker Crumbs	¾ cup	1 cup bread crumbs
Dates	1 lb.	1 ½ cup dates, pitted and cut
Dry Mustard	1 tsp.	1 tbsp. prepared mustard
Flour, Self-Rising	1 cup	1 cup all-purpose flour, ½ tsp. salt, and 1 tsp. baking powder
Herbs, Fresh	1 tbsp.	1 tsp. dried herbs
Milk, Sour	1 cup	1 tbsp. lemon juice or vinegar plus sweet milk to make 1 cup (let stand for 5 minutes)
Milk, Whole	1 cup	½ cup evaporated milk plus ½ cup water
Mini Marshmallows	10	1 large marshmallow
Onion, Fresh	1 small	1 tbsp. instant minced onion
Sugar, Brown	½ cup	2 tbsp. molasses in ½ cup granulated sugar
Sugar, Powdered	1 cup	1 cup granulated sugar plus 1 tsp. cornstarch

Tomato Juice	1 cup	½ cup tomato sauce plus ½ cup water

Equivalency Chart

Food	Quantity	Yield
Apple	1 medium	1 cup
Banana, mashed	1 medium	1/3 cup
Bread	1 ½ slices	1 cup soft crumbs
Bread	1 slice	¼ cup fine, dry crumbs
Butter	1 stick or ¼ lb.	½ cup
Cheese, American, cubed	1 lb.	2 2/3 cups
Cheese, American, grated	1 lb.	5 cups
Cheese, Cream Cheese	3 oz. package	6 2/3 tbsp
Chocolate, bitter	1 square	1 oz.
Cocoa	1 lb.	4 cups
Coconut	1 ½ lb. package	2 2/3 cups
Coffee, ground	1 lb.	5 cups
Cornmeal	1 lb.	3 cups
Cornstarch	1 lb.	3 cups
Crackers, Graham	14 squares	1 cup fine crumbs
Crackers, Saltine	28 squares	1 cup fine crumbs
Egg	4-5 whole	1 cup
Egg, Whites	8 – 10	1 cup
Egg, Yolks	10 – 12	1 cup
Evaporated Milk	1 cup	3 cups whipped
Flour, Cake, sifted	1 lb.	4 ½ cups
Flour, Rye	1 lb.	5 cups
Flour, White, sifted	1 lb.	4 cups
Flour, White un-sifted	1 lb.	3 ¾ cups
Gelatin, flavored	3 ¼ oz.	½ cup
Gelatin, unflavored	¼ oz.	1 tbsp.
Lemon	1 medium	3 tbsp. juice
Marshmallows	16	¼ lb.
Noodles, cooked	8 oz. package	7 cups
Noodles, uncooked	4 oz. (1 ½ cups)	2 – 3 cups cooked
Noodles, Macaroni, cooked	8 oz. cooked	6 cups
Noodles, Macaroni, uncooked	4 oz. (1 ¼ cups)	2 ¼ cups cooked

Noodles, Spaghetti, uncooked	7 oz.	4 cups cooked
Nuts, chopped	¼ lb.	1 cup
Nuts, Almonds	1 lb.	3 ½ cups
Nuts, Walnuts, broken	1 lb.	3 cups
Nuts, Walnuts, unshelled	1 lb.	1 ½ to 1 ¾ cups
Onion	1 medium	½ cup
Orange	3 – 4 medium	1 cup juice
Raisins	1 lb.	3 ½ cups
Rice, Brown	1 cup	4 cups cooked
Rice, Converted	1 cup	3 ½ cups cooked
Rice, Regular	1 cup	3 cups cooked
Rice, Wild	1 cup	4 cups cooked
Sugar, Brown	1 lb.	2 ½ cups
Sugar, Powdered	1 lb.	3 ½ cups
Sugar, White	1 lb.	2 cups
Vanilla Wafers	22	1 cup fine crumbs
Zwieback, crumbled	4	1 cup

Food Quantities
For Large Servings
25 Servings   50 Servings   100 Servings

Beverages:

	25 Servings	50 Servings	100 Servings
Coffee	½ lb. and 1 ½ gallons water	1 lb. and 3 gallons water	2 lb. and 6 gallons water
Lemonade	10 – 15 lemons and 1 ½ gallons water	20 – 30 lemons and 3 gallons water	40 – 60 lemons and 6 gallons water
Tea	1/12 lb. and 1 ½ gallons water	1/6 lb. and 3 gallons water	1/3 lb. and 6 gallons water

Desserts:

Layered Cake	1 12" cake	3 10" cakes	6 10" cakes
Sheet Cake	1 10" x 12" cake	1 12" x 20" cake	2 12" x 20" cakes

Watermelon	37 ½ lb.	75 lb.	150 lb.
Whipping Cream	¾ pint	1 ½ to 2 pints	3 – 4 pints

Ice Cream:

Brick	3 ¼ quarts	6 ½ quarts	13 quarts
Bulk	2 ¼ quarts	4 ½ quarts or 1 ¼ gallons	9 quarts or 2 ½ gallons

Meat, Poultry, or Fish:

Fish	13 lb.	25 lb.	50 lb.
Fish, fillets or steaks	7 ½ lb.	15 lb.	30 lb.
Hamburger	9 lb.	18 lb.	35 lb.
Turkey or Chicken	13 lb.	25 to 35 lb.	50 to 75 lb.
Wieners (beef)	6 ½ lb.	13 lb.	25 lb.

Salads or Casseroles:

Baked Beans	¾ gallon	1 ¼ gallons	2 ½ gallons
Jell-o Salad	¾ gallon	1 ¼ gallons	2 ½ gallons
Potato Salad	4 ¼ quarts	2 ¼ gallons	4 ½ gallons
Scalloped Potatoes	4 ½ quarts or 1 12" x 20" pan	9 quarts or 2 ¼ gallons	18 quarts or 4 ½ gallons
Spaghetti	1 ¼ gallons	2 ½ gallons	5 gallons

Sandwiches:

Bread	50 slices or 3 1 lb. loaves	100 slices or 6 1 lb. loaves	200 slices or 12 1 lb. loaves
Butter	½ lb.	1 lb.	2 lb.
Lettuce	1 ½ heads	3 heads	6 heads
Mayonnaise	1 cup	2 cups	4 cups

Mixed Filling:

Meat, Eggs, Fish	1 ½ quarts	3 quarts	6 quarts
Jam, Jelly	1 quart	2 quarts	4 quarts

Microwave Hints

1. Place an open box of hardened brown sugar in the microwave oven with 1 cup of water. Microwave on high for 1 ½ to 2 minutes for ½ lb. or 2 to 3 minutes for 1 lb.

2. Soften hard ice cream by microwaving it at 30% power. One pint will take 15 to 30 seconds; one quart, 30 to 45 seconds; and one-half gallon, 45 to 60 seconds.

3. To melt chocolate, place ½ lb. in glass bowl or measuring cup. Melt uncovered at 50% power for 3 – 4 minutes; stir after 2 minutes.

4. Soften one 8oz. package of cream cheese by microwaving at 30% power for 2 to 2 ½ minutes. One 3oz. package of cream cheese will soften in 1 ½ to 2 minutes.

5. A 4 ½ oz. carton of whipped topping will thaw in 1 minute on the defrost setting. Whipped topping should be slightly firm in the center, but it will blend well when stirred. Do not over thaw!

6. Soften jell-o that has set up too hard – perhaps you were to chill it until slightly thickened and forgot it. Heat on a low power setting for a very short time.

7. Heat hot packs. A wet fingertip towel will take about 25 seconds. It depends on the temperature of the water used to wet the towel.

8. To scald milk, cook 1 cup for 2 to 2 ½ minutes, stirring once each minute.

9. To make dry bread crumbs, cut 6 slices of bread into ½" cubes. Microwave in 3-quart casserole dish for 6 to 7 minutes, or until dry, stirring after 3 minutes. Crush in the blender.

10. Refresh stale potato chips, crackers, or other snacks of such type by putting a plateful in the microwave

for 30 – 45 seconds. Let stand for 1 minute to crisp. Cereals can also be crisped this way.

11. Nuts will be easier to shell if you place 2 cups of nuts in a 1-quart casserole dish with 1 cup water. Cook for 4 to 5 minutes and the nutmeats will slip out whole after cracking the shell.

12. Stamp collectors can place a few drops of water on a stamp to remove it from an envelope. Heat in the microwave for 20 seconds and the stamp will come off.

13. Using a round dish instead of a square one eliminates overcooked corners in baking cakes.

14. Sprinkle a layer of medium, finely chopped walnuts evenly onto the bottom and side of a ring pan or bundt cake pan to enhance the looks and eating quality. Pour in batter and microwave as recipe directs.

15. Do not salt foods on the surface as it causes dehydration and toughens food. Salt after you remove from the oven unless the recipe calls for using salt in the mixture.

16. Heat left-over custard and use it as frosting for a cake.

17. Melt marshmallow cream. Half of a 7oz. jar will melt in 35 – 40 seconds on high. Stir to blend.

18. To toast coconut, spread ½ cup coconut in a pie plate and cook for 3 – 4 minutes, stirring every 30 seconds after 2 minutes. Watch closely, as it quickly browns.

19. To melt crystallized honey, heat uncovered jar on high for 30 – 45 seconds. If jar is large, repeat.

20. One stick of butter or margarine will soften in 1 minute when microwaved at 20% power.

Calorie Counter

Beverages:

Apple Juice, 6oz.	90
Coffee (black)	0
Cola Type, 12oz.	115
Cranberry Juice, 6oz.	115
Ginger Ale, 12oz.	115
Grape Juice, (from frozen concentrate), 6oz.	142
Lemonade, (from frozen concentrate), 6oz.	85
Milk, protein fortified, 1 cup	105
Milk, Skim, 1 cup	90
Milk, Whole, 1 cup	160
Orange Juice, 6oz.	85
Pineapple Juice, unsweetened, 6oz.	95
Root Beer	150
Tonic (quinine water) 12oz.	132

Breads:

Cornbread, 1 small square	130
Dumplings, 1 med.	70
French Toast, 1 slice	135
Melba Toast, 1 slice	25
Muffins, Blueberry, 1 muffin	110
Muffins, Bran, 1 muffin	106
Muffins, Corn, 1 muffin	125
Muffins, English, 1 muffin	280
Pancakes, 1 (4")	60
Pumpernickel, 1 slice	75
Rye, 1 slice	60
Waffle, 1	216
White, 1 slice	60 - 70
Whole Wheat, 1 slice	55 - 65

Cereals:

Cornflakes, 1 cup	105
Cream of Wheat, 1 cup	120
Oatmeal, 1 cup	148
Rice Flakes, 1 cup	105
Shredded Wheat, 1 biscuit	100
Sugar Krisps, ¾ cup	110

Crackers:

Graham, 1 cracker	15 – 30
Rye Crisp, 1 cracker	35
Saltine, 1 cracker	17 – 20
Wheat Thins, 1 cracker	9

Dairy Products:

Butter or Margarine, 1 tbsp.	100
Cheese, American, 1oz.	100
Cheese, Camembert, 1oz.	85
Cheese, Cheddar, 1oz.	115
Cheese, Cottage Cheese, 1oz.	30
Cheese, Mozzarella, 1oz.	90
Cheese, Parmesan, 1oz.	130
Cheese, Ricotta, 1oz.	50
Cheese, Roquefort, 1 oz.	105
Cheese, Swiss, 1 oz.	105
Cream, light, 1 tbsp.	30
Cream, heavy, 1 tbsp.	55
Cream, sour, 1 tbsp.	45
Hot Chocolate, with Milk, 1 cup	277
Milk Chocolate, 1oz.	145 – 155
Yogurt made w/ whole milk, 1 cup	150 – 165
Yogurt made w/ skimmed milk, 1 cup	125

Eggs:

Fried, 1 large	100
Poached or Boiled, 1 large	75 – 80
Scrambled or in Omelet, 1 large	110 - 130

Fish and Seafood:

Bass, 4oz.	105
Salmon, broiled or baked, 3oz.	155
Sardines, canned in oil, 3oz.	170
Trout, fried, 3 ½ oz.	220
Tuna, in oil, 3oz.	170
Tuna, in water, 3oz.	110

Fruits:

Apple, 1 medium	80 – 100
Applesauce, sweetened, ½ cup	90 – 115
Applesauce, unsweetened, ½ cup	50
Banana, 1 medium	85
Blueberries, ½ cup	45
Cantaloupe, ½ cup	24
Cherries (pitted), raw, ½ cup	40
Grapefruit, ½ medium	55
Grapes, ½ cup	35 – 55
Honeydew, ½ cup	55
Mango, 1 medium	90
Orange, 1 medium	65 – 75
Peach, 1 medium	35
Pear, 1 medium	60 – 100
Pineapple, fresh, ½ cup	40
Pineapple, canned in syrup, ½ cup	95
Plum, 1 medium	30
Strawberries, fresh, ½ cup	30

Strawberries, frozen and sweetened, ½ cup	120 – 140
Tangerine, 1 large	39
Watermelon, ½ cup	42

Meat and Poultry:

Beef, Ground (lean), 3oz.	185
Beef, Roast, 3oz.	185
Chicken, broiled, 3oz.	115
Lamb Chop (lean), 3oz.	175 – 200
Steak, Sirloin, 3oz.	175
Steak, Tenderloin, 3oz.	174
Steak, Top Round, 3oz.	162
Turkey, dark meat, 3oz.	175
Turkey, white meat, 3oz.	150
Veal, Cutlet, 3oz.	156
Veal, Roast, 3oz.	76

Nuts:

Almonds, 2 tbsp.	105
Cashews, 2 tbsp.	100
Peanuts, 2 tbsp.	105
Peanut Butter, 1 tbsp.	95
Pecans, 2 tbsp.	95
Pistachios, 2 tbsp.	92
Walnuts, 2 tbsp.	80

Pasta:

Macaroni or Spaghetti, cooked, ¾ cup	115

Salad Dressings:

Blue Cheese, 1 tbsp.	70
French, 1 tbsp.	65
Italian, 1 tbsp.	80
Mayonnaise, 1 tbsp.	100
Olive Oil, 1 tbsp.	124
Russian, 1 tbsp.	70

Salad Oil, 1 tbsp.	120

Soups:

Bean, 1 cup	130 – 180
Beef Noodle, 1 cup	70
Bouillon and Consommé, 1 cup	30
Chicken Noodle, 1 cup	65
Chicken with Rice, 1 cup	50
Minestrone, 1 cup	80 – 150
Split Pea, 1 cup	145 – 170
Tomato with Milk	170
Vegetable	80 - 100

Vegetables:

Asparagus, 1 cup	35
Broccoli, cooked, ½ cup	25
Cabbage, cooked, ½ cup	15 – 20
Carrots, cooked, ½ cup	25 – 30
Cauliflower, ½ cup	10 – 15
Corn (kernels), ½ cup	70
Green Beans, 1 cup	30
Lettuce, shredded, ½ cup	5
Mushrooms, canned, ½ cup	20
Onions, cooked, ½ cup	30
Peas, cooked, ½ cup	60
Potato, baked, 1 medium	90
Potato, chips, 8 – 10	100
Potato, Mashed, w/ milk & butter, 1 cup	200 - 300
Spinach, 1 cup	40
Tomato, raw, 1 medium	25
Tomato, cooked, ½ cup	30

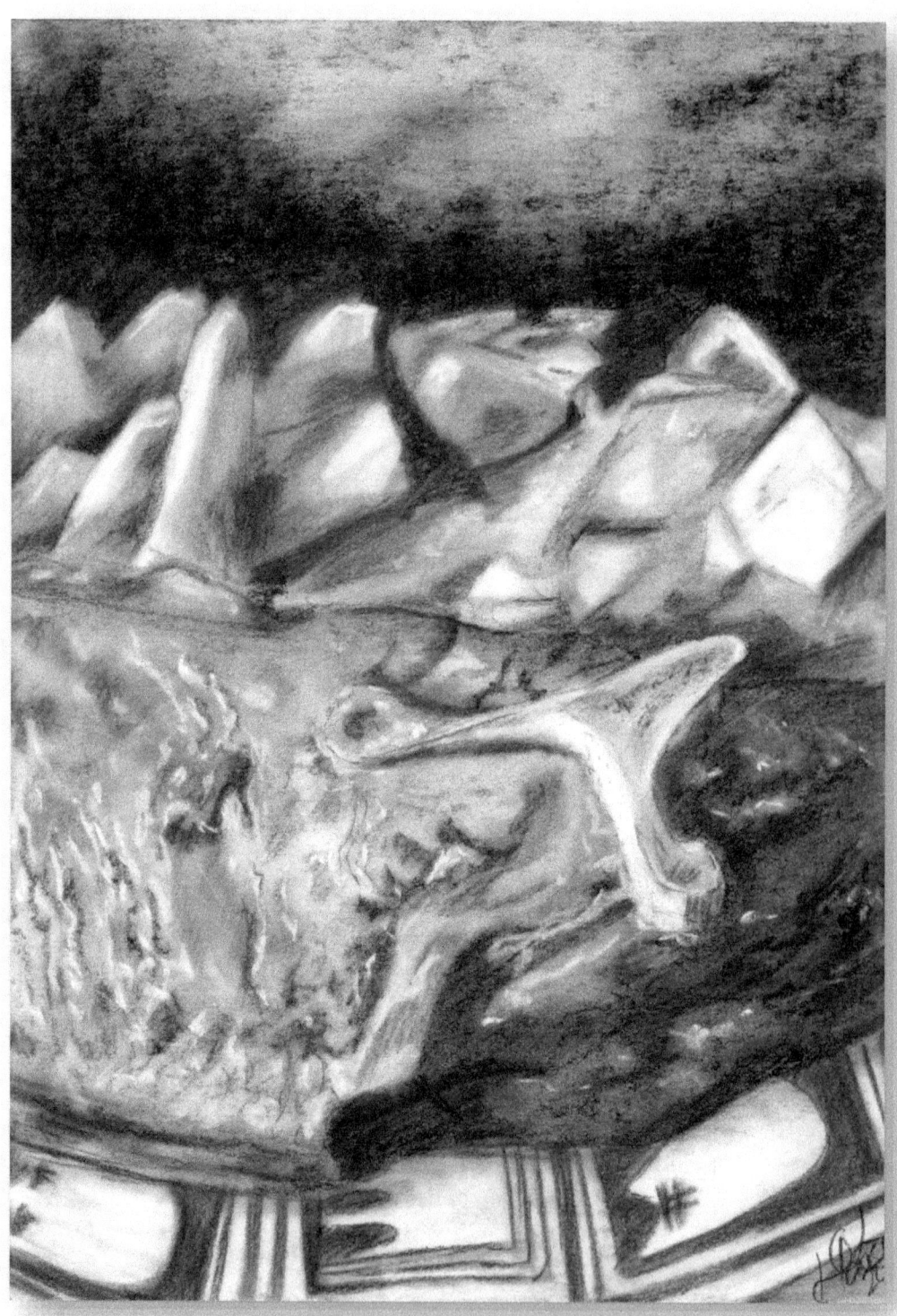

Cooking Terms

Appetizer: A small serving of food served before or as the first course of a meal.

Aspic: A transparent jelly, usually meat, which has been boiled down to become firm when cold.

Au Gratin: Topped with crumbs and/or cheese and browned in oven or under broiler.

Au Jus: Served in its own juices.

Baste: To moisten foods during cooking with pan drippings or special sauce in order to add flavor and prevent drying.

Batter: A mixture of flour or liquid that can be beaten or stirred.

Bisque: A thick cream soup.

Blanch: To place fruits or nuts in boiling water to remove skins, also to dip vegetables in boiling water in preparation for freezing, canning or drying.

Bouillabaisse: A chowder made from several varieties of fish and wine.

Bouillon: Clear soup made from lean beef or chicken.

Braise: To brown meat or vegetables in hot fat, then to cook slowly in small amount of liquid.

Caramel: Burnt sugar syrup used for coloring and flavoring. Also, a chewy candy.

Chicory: A plant root that is cut into slices, dried and roasted into coffee. The plant leaves are used for salad and sometimes call curly endive.

Cider: The juice from pressed apples used as a beverage or to make vinegar.

Clarify: To make a liquid clear by adding beaten egg white and egg shells. The egg coagulates in hot liquid and cloudiness adheres to it. The liquid is then strained.

Cobbler: A fruit pie with a rich biscuit dough made in a deep-dish.

Cocktail: An appetizer served before or as the first course of a meal. An alcoholic beverage served before the dinner; or cut shellfish with tart sauce served at the start of a meal.

Cracklings: Crisp particles left after fat has been fried out.

Cream: To soften a fat, especially butter, by beating it at room temperature. Butter and sugar are often creamed together, making a smooth, soft paste.

Crimp: To seal the edges of a two-crust pie either by pinching them at intervals with the fingers or by pressing them together with the tongs of a fork.

Croquettes: Chopped meat held together by eggs, shaped and dipped into crumbs, then fried.

Crudités: An assortment of raw vegetables (i.e. carrots, broccoli, celery, mushrooms) that is served as a hors d'oeuvre, often accompanied by a dip.

Degrease: To remove fat from the surface of stews, soups, or stock. It's usually cooled in the refrigerator so that fat hardens and is easily removed.

Dough: A mixture of flour and liquid that is stiff enough to be kneaded.

Dredge: To coat lightly with flour, cornmeal, etc.

Drippings: Liquids resulting from meat being cooked.

Entrée: The main course of a meal.

Fold: To incorporate a delicate substance such as whipped cream or beaten egg whites, into another substance without releasing air bubbles. A spatula is used to gently bring part of the mixture from the bottom of the bowl to the top. The process is repeated, while slowly rotating the bowl, until the ingredients are thoroughly blended.

Fondue: A dish made of cheese, eggs, etc.

Fritters: Vegetables or fruit covered with batter then fried in deep fat.

Frosting: A sugar that has been cooked and used to cover cakes, and other foods.

Giblets: The liver, gizzard or heart of poultry.

Ginger: An aromatic, pungent root sold fresh, dried or ground, May be used in pickles, preserves, cakes, cookies, puddings, soups, pot roasts.

Glace: Ice or glossed over. Meats are glazed by covering with concentrated stocks or jellies.

Glaze: To cover with a glossy coating, such as a melted and somewhat diluted jelly for fruit desserts.

Grate: Cut into tiny particles, using small holes of grater.

Hors d'oeuvres Tart, salty or crisp foods served as appetizers.

Infusion: Liquid extracted from tea, herbs or coffee.

Julienne: To cut vegetables, fruits, or cheeses into match-shaped silvers.

Knead: To place dough on flat surface and work it, pressing down with knuckles, then fold, repeating several times.

Legumes: The seeds of certain plants, as peas, beans, peanuts, and lentils.

Macedoine: A mixture of fruits or vegetables.

Marjoram: May be used both green and dry for flavoring soups and ragouts, and in stuffing for all meats and fish.

Marinate: To allow food to stand in a liquid in order to tenderize or to add flavor.

Meuniere: Dredged with flour and sautéed in butter.

Mince: To chop food into very small pieces.

Mornay: A white sauce containing cheese.

Mince: To cut foods in very fine pieces.

Oregano: Whole or ground, strong aromatic odor, used with tomato sauces, pizza and veal dishes.

Parboil: To boil until partially cooked; to blanch. Usually final cooking in a seasoned sauce follows this procedure.

Pare: To remove the outermost skin of a fruit or vegetable.

Peel: Strip off outer covering (oranges).

Piquant: A sharp sauce.

Poach: To cook gently in hot liquid kept just below the boiling point.

Puree: To mash foods by hand by rubbing through a sieve or food mill, or by whirling in a blender or food processor until perfectly smooth.

Refresh: To run cold water over food that has been parboiled in order to stop the cooking process quickly.

Sauté: To cook and/or brown food in a small quantity of hot shortening.

Scald: To heat to just below the boiling point, when tiny bubbles appear at the edge of the saucepan.

Simmer: To cook in liquid just below the boiling point. The surface of the liquid should be barely moving, broken from time to time by slowly rising bubbles.

Steep: to let food stand in hot liquid in order to extract or to enhance flavor, like tea in hot water or poached fruit in sugar syrup.

Tarragon: Leaves have a hot, pungent taste. Valuable to use in all salads and sauces. Used to flavor vinegar.

Toss: To combine ingredients with a repeated lifting motion.

Whip: To beat rapidly in order to incorporate air and produce expansion, as in heavy cream or egg whites.

Also Available from G.W. Mullins creator of
The Southern Mountain Kitchen

The Southern Mountain Kitchen Cookbook
Hardback ISBN: 978-1-958221-06-8 and Paperback ISBN:
978-1-958221-07-5. Available worldwide wherever great
books are sold.

www.ingramcontent.com/pod-product-compliance
Lightning Source LLC
Chambersburg PA
CBHW071328120626
46546CB00002B/479